The
Subversive
Job Search

The
Subversive
Job Search

How to Overcome a Lousy Job,
Sluggish Economy, and
Useless Degree to Create
a Six-Figure Career

By Alan Corey

CAREER
PRESS
Pompton Plains, NJ

THE SUBVERSIVE JOB SEARCH
EDITED AND TYPESET BY DIANA GHAZZAWI
Cover design by Howard Grossman
Printed in the U.S.A.

To order this title, please call toll-free 1-800-CAREER-1 (NJ and Canada: 201-848-0310) to order using VISA or MasterCard, or for further information on books from Career Press.

The Career Press, Inc.
220 West Parkway, Unit 12
Pompton Plains, NJ 07444
www.careerpress.com

Library of Congress Cataloging-in-Publication Data
Corey, Alan.
   The subversive job search : how to overcome a lousy job, sluggish economy, and useless degree to create a six-figure career / by Alan Corey.
       pages cm.
   Includes index.
   ISBN 978-1-60163-257-9 -- ISBN 978-1-60163-536-5 (ebook)
       1. Career development. 2. Job hunting. I. Title.
HF5381.C687825 2013
650.14--dc23
                                                    2012047122

I have dedicated this book to you.

Okay listen, if I were you, I'd tell all your friends you've got a book dedicated to you. That's pretty sweet, right? Now each friend that you get to buy the book, this book will *also* be dedicated to him or her! It's up to you. You can be the nice guy here, or you can choose to hog all the glory for yourself. I dedicated it to you because I knew you would do the right thing. (But please don't tell my sister Jill to buy it; I don't want to dedicate this book to her.)

Contents

Introduction

It was a dark and shitty night. Inside the house, a computer screen's blue glow bathed a face in pink and blue, like the colors of a nursery. But it was on a man's face with a five-day stubble and not a baby face, though according to his wife, he was definitely acting like a baby. "No. Nope. Hell no. Shit no. No way. Jesus H. Mothershitterneverinamillionyears."

Sorry to start off so vulgar, but that was my uncensored mindset as I dug through hundreds of job listings online for the fourth week in a row, dismissing each potential occupation as being beneath me. When I occasionally found ones that I liked, I would assume I'm an unqualified applicant, swear uncontrollably, and move on to the next job listing. That mindset didn't serve me well, and now it has also probably earned me the worst opening line to any book ever. Thanks to my economy-based depression, I'm now non-fiction's answer to Edward Bulwer-Lytton[1].

I was in a funk, and not like a James Brown kind of a funk—more like the kind many of you may have experienced before, or are possibly experiencing now, while trying to plot your escape from a dead-end job or even unemployment. This irritable funk of mine has also been known to appear around irrational bosses, impossible-to-please authority figures, or just about any bad situation that doesn't seem to have a quick fix. Bills piling on top of stress on top of bills on top of stress can make my personality a fragile Jenga tower of profanity-packed tirades. If you aren't convinced I had enough reason to have such a "spirited tongue," please let it sink in how far my star had fallen: I was just two years removed from celebrating the release of my first book, *A Million Bucks by 30*, my rags-to-riches tale of how I had achieved a million dollar net worth in just six and half years. And here I was about to turn 31, fully ashamed that I just took a government-mandated job training course so that I could start collecting unemployment checks.

But don't fret! You're reading this book because I found a remedy to my no-income-inspired malediction. Yes, I made my way back on top again. And this time for good. I'm here to share my experiences, my lessons learned, and possibly a few more "creative outbursts" with you. When I reached my financial rock bottom, I decided my only way out of my funk was to set an overly optimistic goal for myself and do whatever I can to achieve it. Unhelpful advice from loved ones of "just find a job" gave me no direction. Eventually I learned, during the course of 18 months, what it took to go from rock bottom to rock-star and from unemployment to a six-figure income. Don't worry, I'll save you the year and a half it took me, and I'll get to the good stuff quickly. With the right moves, you could be in a whole new pay grade in just six months time. I'll not only teach you how to land a job, but I'll also teach you how to get the bonus you deserve, nail down that raise, and talk yourself into a higher-paying position once you get that job. Whether you are currently employed or not, after reading this book, you'll be richer in more ways than one.

My story is meant to inspire and to motivate. If you need to know anything about me, it's that I'm just a regular guy. If I can do it, then you can do it. Yes, I was in a state of deep depression at one point. My savings were depleted. My income had vanished. My skill set (namely, real estate) no longer served a purpose in a collapsing housing economy. I was embarrassed of my predicament. I was ashamed. I was scared. On top of that, I was a new father and gaining new responsibilities daily. The pressure was on. I had to find a job, any job, and that was quickly becoming the hardest thing in the world to do. But I eventually found a way. And so can you.

Though it may seem like I should be a character in a Horatio Alger novel, I didn't achieve my goal because of any special talents or inside connections. I didn't become a well-heeled investment banker, or a high-powered lawyer, or a jet-setting jewel thief, or even get some sweet family-owned business gig. When I decided that I had to do everything I could to land a six-figure career, I definitely didn't know what I was getting into, but I was excited to make it happen.

So how did I do it? Well, you got a whole book to read to find that out! But I'll give you the first step. It's the same one I used in *A Million Bucks by 30*. To begin with, I started setting realistic goals for myself. I decided I was going to do everything I could to earn a six-figure salary. I made a commitment to myself to always be looking for a way to make more money until I've reached my goal. With a $100,000 annual pay day, I knew I could support my family with no problem and have plenty left over. I had never made six-figures working for someone else before. Hell, I'd never made more than a $55,000 salary before. I'd been successful working for myself, but entering the corporate world again was going to be a challenge. With this small goal, it made me face the hard truth that I maybe had to start over at an entry-level job. I needed to do something as I was currently going nowhere by sitting around collecting unemployment checks with a finite end-date. I didn't want to resort to begging and borrowing, so I threw all my efforts into building a career.

In the following chapters, I'll break down exactly how I achieved six-figures from nothing, and the strategies and steps I took along the way. Each chapter will begin with my autobiographical journey of stumbling into a career path, subversively job hopping, and then finding creative ways to increase my salary. These tales will be followed by a "Subversive Job Search 101," a quick recap and highlights of my lessons learned, and a "What You Can Do Today" guideline for taking control of your paycheck. These sections will provide the takeaway lessons from my anecdotes and give you concrete next steps to increase your career prospects. Also scattered throughout the book are "Subversive Job Tips" that provide unique advice to get noticed by taking the extra step in a crowded marketplace. Each chapter will then conclude with "Salary Science," actual studies and research you can use for additional support to get you to where you want to go.

My success getting to a six-figure career wasn't just a chance connection or a moment of luck that would only work for me. It was part strategic networking, part creative thinking, and a large part hard work. Of course, these three ingredients in anybody can lead to serendipitous adventures, so follow my steps to make your own success.

As many of you know, finding a job can be a full-time job in itself, and I made it mine. This is not a get rich quick scheme for the slothful (even though pictures of cute sloths are all the rage on the Internet these days). This is just like anything you want in life: you have to be extremely motivated to make a big change. If you don't have ambition, then you're stuck with exactly what you have. (And I imagine you're probably only reading this book because someone said it's dedicated to you.) But if you do want a change, and you do want a more satisfying career, and you do want more money, I'm here to help.

The title of this book is The Subversive Job Search. Now, I'm not teaching you to form a coup amongst your co-workers to overthrow your boss. Though I have witnessed this, and it failed miserably, resulting in mass firings. Granted, mass firings are much better than mass firing squads, like in a real coup, but still... I'll be turning your job search, and your career, on its head. I'll approach it from a different angle. I'll be teaching you to subtly find a way to stand out and be noticed at the job you do have now. If you don't have a job, I'll inform you how to differentiate yourself from the competition and create bidding wars over your services. And I'll instruct you on how to be a well-paid expert in your field with just a few simple tweaks to your resume.

So if you find yourself constantly swearing because of your paycheck or lack thereof, this book is for you. If your incompetent coworker got a raise and you didn't, this book is for you. If you find yourself in a rut career-wise and don't see a way out, this book is for you. If no one is responding to your resume, or you just aren't sure what step to take next in your career, this book can help you too. Now if you are the lucky sort that is completely happy with life and you just want to make more damn money, this book will also be of assistance (but just don't read it with that annoying smirk on your face the whole time). I learned to get the most out of my income potential quickly, and the point of this book is to show you how you can too.

I hope that by sharing my story, you can draw parallels to your life and experiences and achieve equivalent success. Take my story and apply it to your career. I am just a normal dude with a big dream. Chances are you are above-average with a big dream. You may be educated and qualified, but still struggling to make sense of a career. If so, you are one step ahead of me when I started my journey. Regardless of your scenario, if I can do it, so can you. Good luck on your path to creating your huge pay day, and most of all, have fun! It sure makes the swearing stop. Fudge yeah!

1

Millionaire Mudslide

I hope that after I die, people will say of me, "That guy sure owed me a lot of money."

—Jack Handy

At age 31, this was me:

Week 1: *Sitting at home, unemployed, is awesome!*

Week 2: *Sitting at home, unemployed, is awesome!*

Week 3: *Sitting at home, unemployed, is awesome!*

Week 4: *Sitting at home and unemployed is the worst thing ever in the world. Please someone stab my eyes with a salted spork and kick my teeth in just to give me a different type of pain! I would not wish this horrendous boredom and depression upon my worst enemy (or any previous bosses). Please bosses, call me back and offer me a job! I promise to play slightly less Minecraft on company time!*

So how did I end up here? After all, my parting words in *A Million Bucks by 30* were, "Now at 29, I am in position to no longer have another boss again. I am financially comfortable, with multiple income sources, and I'm free to do as I please."

Now I am binge-eating crow, and it doesn't taste much like chicken—but a lot like burned tires and black feathers. How did I go from making that boastful declaration to requesting culinary eye torture just a year and a half later?

Well, it took a series of life-changing events. Many positive, some negative, some out of my control, but the combinations of them all led to my financial demise.

After "retiring" from my day job a month shy of my 29th birthday, I had envisioned living off the passive rental income I was earning from my house, money from my bar and restaurant, and hopefully some coin from book royalties. And that's exactly how I ended up—passive. Retirement now provided me entire days, entire weeks, and entire months to do as I pleased. I could go to the beach, travel, or just play video games all day. I was living the dream. But that dream quickly turned into a spiraling, bankrupting nightmare.

Like being unemployed, retirement was great for the first three weeks. Then out of nowhere, I became suffocated by boredom and overwhelmed by a sickening funk called depression. As an excuse to leave the house, I would spend three hours at the gym everyday just so I had something to do. (I may have been the first depressed guy ever in great shape. I imagined girls were like, "Damn, that unshowered emo guy's got a sick bod.") I'd be home by noon and just wait for

my friends to get off work at 5 p.m. and pray someone would want to go out that night. (I am fully aware
that I'm probably not gaining your sympathy, but hear
me out.) Everyone I knew had to go to a day job 40
hours a week, so they weren't interested in staying out
at the bars with me until 4 a.m. on a Monday. Or any
other day of the week, for that matter. I had achieved
my million dollar dream, but now that I had a whole
new lifestyle, I found I no longer had anyone to share
it with. So let this be a lesson for all you young future
millionaires out there: don't befriend responsible adults
with goals and dreams of their own. They will continue
to be dedicated, determined, and focused on their goals
even when you aren't. (I suppose if I had befriended the
alternative, they would have just helped me spend my
money faster.)

Yes, I could have volunteered, started a new project,
or found something productive to do, but a depressed
mindset has no motivation. It was hard enough to get
myself to even go to the gym. I probably really be-
longed at a Left Bank café in 1920s Paris, with fellow
expat existentialists bemoaning the banality of bour-
geois existence. As the only 29-year-old I knew with no
daily responsibilities, no deadlines, and endless hours
of the day to burn, I was becoming a waste of flesh. I
couldn't even do retirement right. Surely of all places,
New York City would have other young retirees with
these same rich guy "problems" as me, and we could
be best buds, but I never found someone sharing my
similar utopian pain. Plus, rich twenty-somethings seem

to be such an egotistical and annoying bunch that, had I met one, I probably would have instantly wished for some sort of financial hardship to come their way.

So I started doing something that I had never done before. I became a reckless and aimless retiree by spending money. I started spending money like I had endless riches. I figured I was finally a millionaire and wanted to act like it. I had earned it after all. I started buying drinks for everyone at the bar. Anyone. Also, getting the bills for dinners became a thing. I had a reputation to uphold as the published bloke that was young, rich, and lucky. Why not share the wealth?

I justified it by thinking, "Why did I work so hard for all these years if there wasn't some satisfying reward in the end?" So I kept spending, and it entertained me during this slow period of my life. I was buying my happiness. And then when the spending stopped, the boredom and depression returned. And then I went out and spent some more money to give me something to do. I was in a cycle of blowing money and feeling down, one temporarily canceling out the other. It was a fruitless effort with no lasting satisfaction. (I imagine this is what being a Kardashian is like, but way less money. And way less booty. And minus the depression part. Well, probably nothing like them at all, thankfully.)

During this time, my bar and restaurant was spinning its wheels and just breaking even. Yes, I owned a dive bar and a restaurant, but my state of mind meant I began neglecting it. (Cue the world's smallest violin playing the coolest song you've never heard before.)

The economy had soured, and everyone was in fear it would continue tanking, and it eventually did. Even in NYC, eating out became a luxury, and no one wanted to spend their savings in a dive bar. Because it wasn't earning the extra cash I envisioned it would with my hands-off management, I decided to sell the establishment that helped make me a millionaire. I had fallen out of love with it, and I was ready to move on. I sold it in an extremely down market and then split the pittance I made with my business partner.

Also, I quickly learned that living off book royalties is a feat only achieved by a handful of authors who sell millions of books a year. By comparison, I'll probably never sell 50,000 books in a lifetime. (You'll know when I do because I'll write 50,000 *Books by 90!*) I did have potentially lucrative movie, TV shows, and more in the works, but nothing came from them besides countless meetings that all ended with no approved budget. The media industry was also counting its pennies and tightening its pocketbooks. Its reasoning for not moving forward was that during our current depression, people wanted to turn to their TVs to forget about things like a sagging economy, money management, and personal finance. Apparently, depressed people want to watch *really* depressing things, like *Toddlers and Tiaras, Here Comes Honey Boo Boo,* or any other crap on TLC. (And to think TLC was once The Learning Channel.) Obviously I disagreed and thought this is the moment demand for personal finance would be the highest, but I finally came to the understanding it was out of my control and that things weren't looking bright financially speaking on that front either.

But then came good news. I met and married the girl of my dreams. (She married the man of her reality.) We both wanted a special ceremony and preferred a destination wedding. We came up with a $10,000 budget for the entire wedding and made the numbers work for us to have it as a week-long affair in Costa Rica. We had about 40 friends and family join us for the best time we've ever had. Returning to the United States as an officially wedded couple, we both wanted one thing: to start a new life in a new house.

With five months notice, I kicked out my roommates and tenants from my two-family house (and their monthly passive income along with it) to do a complete gut renovation of my only remaining asset. As attached to it as I was, I couldn't live in a bachelor pad anymore. The globes of dust balls, the permanent bath tub rings, and the floor-to-ceiling stack of discarded boxes had somehow now lost their allure. It was time to be mature! Like many home renovations, this project was an instant money pit. A starting budget of $250,000 eventually doubled due to hidden surprises found under every floor and behind every wall, along with countless project delays, and of course, the excitement of upgrades. "Might as well do it spectacular if we're going to do it," was my idiotic refrain. (Not so mature!) So yes, I had a dream home in the end, but this dream alone cost me over half of my net worth and completely wiped out every penny in my savings, checking, and investment accounts. My only asset now was a newly renovated home in a historic housing market collapse. I felt like a King of Garbage Mountain.

Throughout my financial implosion, I did find ways to earn a few bucks here and there. Because I "retired" and was not laid off, I could not collect government-issued unemployment checks like my other jobless friends received. So income from my day job just completely ceased the day I walked away as a tech support operator. What did work in my favor was that I happened to retire right about when the company hit a huge growth spurt. They called me and begged me to return as a contractor as they were overwhelmed with work. I accepted and temporarily worked as a contractor for a few months. I was paid hourly at twice the rate I was making when I worked as a full-time employee. But I was too proud to ask for a full-time job back. I couldn't admit it to myself that retirement was the dumbest thing I could have ever done. Instead with this contractor setup, I was able to finagle myself into working overtime pretty much every week just to make sure I made ends meet. They loved having me there as much as possible, and I definitely needed the money. This contracting gig was a saving grace for three months, until the company was bought and I was made redundant. Although I hated to see it end, I learned a lot about early retirement, contracting, and negotiating when you have leverage. I also learned the lesson that I shouldn't be ashamed to come crawling back to my job. As they say, shit happens. I should have

taken that shit and turned it into compost to reap beau-
tiful rewards. Instead, my own internal shit cost me the
chance to get my $55,000 gig back.

So I was paycheck-less once again. Conveniently
enough, this was just about the same time my wife and
I became pregnant. (Well, her more so than me.) As my
need to take care of my soon-to-be expanding family
kicked into high gear, I went on a resume-bombing session and spammed every job listing I could. I had not job
hunted in almost a decade, this was a whole new world
for me. My tech support job was my first real job out of
college, and I'd had it ever since. Besides my tech support
experience, my resume was filled with random entrepreneurial endeavors I did for extra cash when the economy
was booming. Those gigs had long dried up. Now I just
needed any job, so I didn't even bother reading the online listings. I figured it was just law of averages on my
side that there had to be a fit somewhere for me, eventually. So I sent my resume everywhere. For everything.

After a few weeks, I actually got one interview that
was completely below my skill set, but I needed some sort
of income, so I went to check it out. It was for a customer service manager job at an online electronics company.
After a lengthy interview with the CEO, I got offered
the job and spent the next week subversively negotiating
the best incentive-laced contract ever. I was really proud
of myself. The bad news was that my salary was for
$40,000—the same starting salary I had nine years prior.
That was all they could offer, but I was quickly building
a good rapport with the CEO, and we both knew he was
getting a good deal if I accepted the job.

When an interview con- **Subversive Job Tip**
cludes, thank the person for
his or her time and control
the next steps by providing an actionable item on
your part. Asking "Do you mind if I follow up
with you next Tuesday?" not only pegs you as a
go-getter, but makes your follow-up much easier,
as it is now anticipated. That follow-up should be
whatever is four business days later. Bonus points:
Imply you are in high demand during an interview. Use "I know you are interviewing others,
and I'm interviewing as well. Do you mind if I
follow up with you next Tuesday, as I'll probably
have to make a decision fairly quickly?" When
you follow up, if the person is still undecided,
mention a fake third-round interview happening
elsewhere and tell him or her you'll follow up
again in four more days.

After some prying, I figured out his main concern. The
company's online approval ratings on various e-commerce
platforms were directly related to sales. The better customer service ratings they had, the more orders they received. Because online retail was a highly competitive
business, a few percentage points could be a difference
between hundreds of thousand dollars by the end of the
year.

So I bargained with him that if I got customer service ratings up from the current 93 percent to 97 percent within my first year, they retroactively pay me as if I had been paid $75,000 from day 1? We both knew that would be worth it to the company, and I felt like the CEO thought that was an impossible task. Obviously, I didn't know how possible or impossible the task was, but I knew I needed more than $40,000, and I wasn't sure how easily the company gave raises, promotions, or bonuses. I pitched my proposal and crossed my fingers.

After thinking it over, the CEO, who was very skeptical, eventually agreed to my retroactive salary pitch. He said I reminded him of himself when he was "young and hungry." I was more accurately old and hungry, but I didn't correct him. I returned the next day to work out the nitty-gritty of the contract. His stipulations were that I couldn't increase the staff count, I had to accept a few additional responsibilities outside of customer service without neglecting my main customer service responsibilities, I couldn't take a day off during the holiday rush between Thanksgiving and New Year's, and I still had to be employed as the customer service manager within one year of signing my employment contract (so I would not take a new role within, leave the company, etc.).

I accepted and jumped at the challenge ahead of me, and immediately went to work at reaching my customer-approval goal. Like anything, if I can turn this into a game, it becomes fun. And there is always a need to find day jobs fun. Getting to 97 percent was a high-stakes game: if I won, I had a $35,000 bonus at the end, almost doubling my salary. That's motivation right there!

My background in tech support trained me well for this job, as I knew customers wanted to hear sorry and be comforted whenever a call came in. Upset users of your product are a forgiving bunch, if you give them the chance. The current operation had a ridiculous policy of "never say sorry" that the CEO had implemented years before. According to Ali MacGraw in *Love Story*, love means never having to say you're sorry, but customer service? That's unheard of. My CEO thought sorry meant you are admitting wrong doing and the customer would mention all the wrong things you did in their online feedback. In reality, the feedback would be positive, because you had stepped up and took responsibility.

I eventually undermined, changed, or removed all of the other archaic, illogical, and unnecessary processes and procedures he had the customer support team doing. From the get-go, and rightfully so, he was nervous of me altering this highly important aspect of his company. Because of this, I never really earned his trust and compliance, even as our support ratings were drastically improving. To get anything done I had to make changes, train the team, and then keep it from the CEO. If he found out about my changes, I'd ask for his forgiveness later. I learned quickly that asking for his permission upfront to make a change would never get approval. I found that the biggest obstacle in me getting my big payday at the end was going to be him (whether intentional or not). We butted heads over every single thing he found out about. I spent many a late night in his office explaining myself and my actions. I was on a mission that would benefit both of us, if he'd just give me the time and freedom.

With my hard-fought changes to seemingly obvious improvements, it took only three months to get to 97 percent approval rating. I asked for a review and showed up in his office with detailed spreadsheets, positive emails from customers, and response time stats showing how great we were doing. He pointed out the contract still specified I had to take additional responsibilities, be working there for a year, and be around during the holiday rush when he needed me the most. I agreed that is what the contract specified and took on some additional projects he assigned me on the spot. For the most part, the customer service team was on auto-pilot with my new changes and they didn't need my oversight much anymore, so I went full throttle with the new assignments, counting the days until my big pay day.

Eventually November and December came and went with no time off, and our support approval ratings were now up to 98 percent, above what I had committed to doing. I was ready for my year-end review. I had worked there 364 days and was so excited to get his congratulations (he's not one to congratulate often). Of course, I really just wanted to get his approval to retroactively increase my salary. It was going to be the best New Year's present, and there was no doubt I had earned every milestone laid on in my contract.

The CEO was genuinely curious about how I was able to achieve higher than expected ratings, as he had done everything in his power to improve it prior to hiring me. I was happy to recap all the changes I made. I shared what worked and didn't work with his prior policies. Thinking he was ecstatic with the success, I was caught off-guard when the CEO gave me the world's worst stink eye and then flipped his lid. (If you've never witnessed a classic stink eye lid-flip, consider yourself lucky.) He couldn't believe I pretty much replaced his entire and unwieldy workflow in customer support. He couldn't believe that after several written warnings of being tardy to an employee that he had hired prior to me, that I fired him because he didn't show up for work for six days in a row. (Although the firing instantly increased team morale, productivity, and responsibility.) And he was super-pissed to find out I not only allowed, but encouraged, the customer service team to say sorry when we made a mistake. My bad.

That meeting eventually escalated into a heated one-sided argument. I remained cool, calm-headed, and confident that I did the right thing. Emotions in business are never a good thing, and I kept calm during the whole tongue-lashing he was giving me. The only thing on my mind really was just to get the $35,000 approval, and I needed to assuage the argument until then. However he was so upset, even with the positive results

I had produced, that he demoted me on the spot and stripped me of my title of customer service manager. He claimed that because I was not the customer service manager anymore, that voided the contract. If I wanted this position back, I had to change everything back to his old way of doing things and then he'd reconsider the retroactive salary payment. In a matter of seconds, my huge payday evaporated in thin air.

Now I'm not sure if his decision was premeditated or it was a culmination of a year's worth of head-butting, but I refused to accept his offer to work my way back to customer service manager. I wanted no part of undoing all the constructive work I had done over the past year. Plus I couldn't work for someone who didn't respect the positive work I was indeed doing. Yes, he's the CEO and he can be the demise of his own company, but I was sick of trying to save the company from him. It might have been my pride getting in the way again, but I stood my ground and told him I wouldn't accept his offer.

Because I refused to change things back to his way, he fired me on the spot and ended the meeting. I guess I couldn't blame him; the business wasn't exactly thriving in the downturn and a $35,000 bonus to an undermining employee is a tough pill to swallow. I did do things without his knowledge, but as the manager, I felt like I had the ability to make those decisions. In short, it took just shy of a year to grasp it wasn't the greatest fit. The silver lining, if there was one, was that I was now able to start collecting government-issued unemployment checks. It was a measly amount, but at least it was *something*. It was easier than having no income at all. And all too soon my joblessness funk and my foul-mouth swearing at my computer screen returned. I felt like a failure again, and my depression started to creep back.

So there you have it. A depression-fueled spending rage, an out-of-control home renovation project, and an extreme falling-out with a boss is how an idiotic kid can blow a million bucks and two good job opportunities within 18 months, and end up on unemployment assistance. I see how athletes, rappers, and other celebrities get in these messes now, and I feel their pain. It's a synergy of things that contribute to one's financial demise, not just one thing. And believe me, it's something I'll never get into again. (Note to self: Alan, you do not like eating crow. Even with sriracha.)

I take full blame for blowing away most of my wealth. The root cause was depression, and it took me a long time to admit it and seek help. Also, I shouldn't be embarrassed to work in jobs that I consider beneath me. A job is a job, appreciate what you have. A superiority complex does not pay well, unless you plan to be an emperor. After seeing a therapist, I finally was able to notice a brighter side to things. I was able to pick up my fractured self, reconstruct a new life, and start setting some goals again. First one up was a vague goal, but it was better than no goal at all. And it was slightly more descriptive than a goal of just finding a job. The new goal I made for myself would be that I wanted to find a job that paid $100,000. That's it. And well, if possible, I hoped to achieve it in anything other than customer service. That occupation had burned me out. If I succeeded in reaching a six-figure pay day, I pictured myself on cloud nine and basking in ever-lasting happiness. I had that happiness once before when I was close to reaching my million-dollar net worth. I was now jonesing for that same glee to return. Although $100,000 was my ultimate goal, I knew I would have to work up to it incrementally. I did not have the skill set or mind frame to be paid six-figures at the moment, but I would do anything it took to get there. First it meant getting to work on finding work, and then I'd figure it out from there. I would try to finagle a raise at every opportunity I could. There had to be a way to skyrocket to the top of the career ladder, I just had to find a backdoor, a loophole, or maybe both. Subversion was my specialty, so I knew I had to employ it here too. I had worked too hard to have thrown away everything I earned, and this time I wanted to prove it to myself that I could do it again.

Subversive Job Search 101

So yeah, my life wasn't so rough during retirement with endless free time, but it was a different life. And one I didn't like. I have no one to blame but myself for burning through all my money. Looking back, I should have at least taken the late, bankrupt soccer star George Best's money management philosophy. After his career ended, he was often quoted saying, "I spent 90 percent of my money on women, drink, and fast cars. The rest I wasted." I couldn't laugh at my current predicament, as I wasted mine on chasing happiness. Depression was indeed the factor of my demise, and it took me awhile to admit it to myself. If you find yourself in a similar situation, don't ignore it. You wouldn't try to fix a broken arm by yourself, so don't try to drink, or medicate, or outspend your way out of depression by yourself either. It just doesn't work. Therapists spend years in school to gain the expertise to help you, so allow them to help you.

Because I had worked so hard to create this idyllic situation, I felt like everything would now be perfect. I had one goal since the age of 22, and that was to have a million bucks by the age of 30. While doing everything I could to reach the goal, I was content, happy, and determined. But having reached my milestone, I became directionless, stagnant, and depressed. For seven years, all my energy, thoughts, and motivations were based on one thing only: would this make me a millionaire? Now that I didn't have that constant thought on my mind, I didn't know what to do with myself, and I was having cabin fever in my brand new home. I was harshly taught a lesson that a life moving nowhere is no life at all. Luckily, I had relearned that goal-setting helps keep me moving. You too should always be working toward something. Anything. And hopefully it will keep you from making the same mistakes I made.

Although it didn't work out in the end for me, it's on you to get creative during salary negotiations. Your boss is expecting some back-and-forth at the bargaining table, so don't just acquiesce to your first salary offer. The CEO is trying to save a buck, so you have to work to make that buck back. Asking for a $35,000 bonus when your salary is $40,000 is unheard of and will likely get you tossed out of the room. But phrasing it differently gets you a little farther and makes it much easier for a boss to digest. The key is to put a monetary value on the tasks that need to get done. Is your company hiring for a newly created position or trying to replace someone that has left? If so, grab some of those responsibilities and see if you can get it into your salary and job description for an extra pay day. You could phrase it like this: "Yo Boss, I know how to save the company $20k! I don't think we need to hire someone to take over our company blog just because Betty left. Let's take that new blogger's salary of $40,000 and cut it in half. The company gets $20,000 back. With the other half, the company spends $5,000 getting me the training I need to do it. And if I do a good job, and maintain high quality on my current responsibilities, how about in three months we talk about me getting a $15,000 raise. It would be a monetary win for the both of us. Would that work for you?"

If possible, make sure that your added responsibilities don't translate into longer hours in the office. The more I take on, the more efficient my work gets. I always do my best to never bring my work home from the office. Being efficient at the office creates a nice work/life balance that we Americans need to learn how to master. But the trick to getting a raise this way is identifying what responsibilities are unassigned, figure out what those responsibilities are worth, and then try to claim them for yourself with increased pay. Look for upcoming projects, internal job postings, and people leaving, and you can help earn yourself a raise by being proactive. If you aren't doing it, someone else probably is. Having a discussion like this with your boss is a way to set clearly defined objectives for those extra tasks with matching rewards. In the end you'll have more skills, you will have shown initiative, and you're saving the company money. Who wouldn't want to reward an employee like that?

Take note, having documentation is a huge boon for you in all salary negotiations. Throughout the year I had printed out spreadsheets and statistics showing how much I was improving customer support. In addition, I also printed out the most positive e-mail replies from customers as official proof our customers were benefiting from my changes. With a pile of evidence in front of you, it's hard to deny that you are a positive force within the company and one that should be rewarded. That is, unless you have a myopic grudge-holding penny-pinching CEO (they are rumored to exist).

I got fired on day 364 of a one-year contract and lost $35,000. Make sure any verbal commitments you get are worked into your contract, and then hold your year-end review on day 366! It could be a costly mistake otherwise. I didn't sue or pursue any action to get my back pay. It would have probably cost me as much money as I would have gotten back. I blamed myself that I didn't put in the effort for the job search upfront. I was too egotistical to follow the system the CEO had worked so hard to put in place. Plus, I didn't really understand the environment that I was getting myself into. I blindly sent my resume off to any ol' job listing, and only one person called me back after several months of work and close to a thousand applications submitted. Without doing my homework upfront, I set myself up to be taken advantage of. I would have said yes to anything. I still had a lot to learn about applying for a job. And learning how to find a job was where my focus had to be now. I definitely knew how to talk myself into an increase in income once I got offered a job. If I could only get a perfect-fitting job coupled with my crafty salary negotiations, I could be able to parlay that into a lucrative career. I now had to start a subversive job search to get me there.

What You Can Do Today

Set a goal for your career today. The best way to go nowhere fast is to have nowhere to go. If you have a vision of yourself in a better life, earning a bigger paycheck, or just working in a different job, then make it your ultimate priority. And then EVERY decision thereafter is easy for you. Ask yourself, does this directly help me achieve my goal? If the answer is yes, then do it. If the answer is no, then don't do it. Plain and simple. With this decision model you come closer to your goal and all your decision making is done for you. No more running in place—or going backward!

More than 30 years ago, George T. Doran created the ultimate five steps to goal-setting, which have been amended, extended, and rephrased by many, while maintaining Doran's original idea. To this day, his basic mnemonic SMART is considered the best way to set, track, and achieve your goals.

S—Specific. You must identify the who, what, when, and where of your goal.

M—Measureable. How will you know when you have accomplished it?

A—Attainable. How are you going to do it? Identify the steps you are going to take.

R—Relevant. Is it a realistic goal given your skill set and current situation?

T—Time-framed. What am I going to do today to help me toward this goal? What am I going to do next week? When will the ultimate goal be completed?

When you identify and spell out these five components of your goal, it instantly makes it more achievable. "Making a six-figure salary" is a vague and loose goal that is hard to picture, and thus, hard to achieve. Let's say I had instead defined a goal of "making a six-figure salary as a director of a customer service center with

100+ phone reps within four years," it now becomes a much clearer and achievable goal. I now know not only what the goal is, but the sub-steps to getting there are instantly revealed to me. First, I would need experience managing a 50-person call center before I could manage a 100-person call center. I would either have to get a new job at a bigger company that has more phone reps or grow my current team of 10 by a huge amount. Probably the best plan would be to find a way to job hop to a bigger position every two years. Things start falling into place for you with a descriptive goal, and it makes moving forward career wise that much easier. Just the simple act of writing down your goal using the SMART format can highlight your next steps so you never feel lost or stuck in your career again. SMART, it's better than DUMB.

Salary Science

One last note here about the importance of the right mindset to get you paid what you deserve. You are not the only one unhappy or unemployed. Stubbornness or being too embarrassed to make changes in your habits can lead you right into depression. And if you are depressed, you definitely aren't going to make as much money as you should.

Having depression and even overcoming depression can have lasting effects. Jason Fletcher of the Yale School of Public Health did a study[1] on the effects of being depressed as a teenager. Studying data during a

13-year period, he found people that were depressed as teenagers and overcame it still end up making approximately 20 percent less than their peers and are 5 percent more likely to be unemployed than their peers once they reach adulthood. As if depression wasn't already depressing enough, it costs you money too! Being aware of symptoms and getting treatment for depression early are some of the biggest opportunities to secure a larger paycheck for you now and in the future. And if you think you can cowboy-up and Toby Keith your way through depression, a study[2] by Steven Stack and Jim Gundlack suggests otherwise. They were able to make a correlation that cities with the largest airtime devoted to country music end up having the highest suicide rates. So there you have it, country music is bad for your soul. On the other hand, I'm wondering how healthy it is that Pandora only suggests new rap songs to me because they have cash-obsessed lyrics. Maybe it's time to start a socially conscious folk-rock channel.

As for trying to buy your happiness, a Northwestern University study[3] found that people who place high value on consumerism by buying high-status or luxury items are more likely to be depressed, anxious, and anti-social. There is now empirical evidence that acquiring high wealth or high status to impress others is a losing game. I agree with Oprah Winfrey when she said, "be thankful for what you have; you'll end up having more. If you concentrate on what you don't have, you will never, ever have enough." Maybe that's why Oprah gives away all those "CAAAAAARS!!!" (And that now makes two books in a row in which I quote Oprah Winfrey. I'm quoting Oprah more than her best friend Gayle King. Now where do I turn my man card in?)

It's best to pursue a higher net worth for a purpose such as traveling, opening a business, or raising a family than it is for the sake of increasing your image, status, or to keep up with the Joneses. Believe me, there is always going to be someone that has more stuff than you. Those Joneses are old money. Psychologists Leaf Van Boven and Thomas Gilovich's work[4] has found that spending money on experiences such as vacations, acquiring new skills, and traveling are more rewarding to a person's happiness than spending money on products. Do you look back more fondly on your sky-diving trip or on getting that new car stereo? A University of Chicago and University of Wisconson study[5] also confirms this as they believe the best way to generate happiness is to spend your disposable income on leisure activities such as vacations, entertainment, and sports. Spending it on these items helps increase social bonds and positive memories, boosting your happiness. Products eventually break and become obsolete, making things not so cheerful.

According to Harvard Business Professor Michael Norton,[6] spending your money on others is also a sure fire way to increase your happiness. He was intrigued that lottery winners end up worse in life than if they didn't win at all. He found that they tend to insulate themselves with a big house in a new neighborhood behind big walls. This makes them more anti-social and distances them from family and friends. It's the same reason "gated community" is an oxymoron. He noted that everyone lottery winners know start asking them for hand-outs, so they cut off communication. That means the money they do spend is purely on themselves in the pursuit of acquiring material goods, which makes them feel selfish. Similar to my own spending cycle of my newfound riches, I was emotional-spending money just like they end up doing. The lottery winners eventually become lottery whiners, by creating more debt for themselves while simultaneously losing most of their friends. His research has found that the simple act of buying things for others, no matter the value, makes one happier than spending money on oneself. His research has also shown that when someone is given money to spend on a team member, whether a sales team or a dodge ball team, it will increase the productivity of the team. If someone is given the same amount of money to just spend on themselves, the team's productivity actually decreased. It didn't matter if it was five bucks or 20 bucks; it was the simple act of buying something for others that helped increase team morale and productivity.

Take heed, though, regarding this research: materialism does not improve your life, and depression can financially ruin it. If I knew these two things, I would have saved a million bucks!

2

The Resume
Jungle

Boxing was the only career where I
wouldn't have to start at the bottom.
I had a good resume.

—Sugar Ray Leonard

As I now began shedding my self-defeating thoughts
and having curbed my propensity to swear at my computer monitor, I decided to take job-hunting from a
different approach. There had to be a better way than
pissed off resume-bombing every listing with a scowl
on my face. I decided I had to change one thing to make
this soul-numbing task somewhat bearable. I was going
to be completely optimistic instead. The economy was
now even worse, and unemployment numbers across
the United States were rising, so getting a job was now
even more difficult. I had to believe I was the best to
stand out. I hoped that now my unbridled optimism
would shine through on the other side of the screen
and get me a job. Just maybe optimism alone could turn

average into above-average. Optimistic resume-bombing would at least be a more pleasing experience. I still didn't know what else to do to find a job, but it felt like I was headed in the right direction with a simple change in 'tude.

Now we all wish we could put "earned a million bucks by age 30," "published author," or even "owned a bar and restaurant" on our resume, right? These phrases not only set you apart from other applicants, but they clearly show you have "a successful track record" and are "very entrepreneurial," key requirements found in many job listings. It would also highlight how you are an accomplished jack-of-all-trades and underscore that you are one determined mofo, just one lucky son of a bitch, or possibly both. Who wouldn't want to be associated with (or even better, work with) a sure success, a man who fought The Man and won? I would definitely want him or her on my team. I was as good as it gets.

So, I had it easy. Agreed. My resume spoke for itself, and it was a free pass to any corporate gig, even in a down economy. Why would any hiring manager go with some unproven, unknown underdog when you could get the undefeated heavyweight of an applicant right here? I was now thinking highly of myself; shedding my funk by doing this making life much better.

So I was once again off applying for anything and everything under the sun, any job that seemed somewhat interesting to me or that I thought I would be good at got sent my resume. I sent it off for jobs that pay $50k, jobs that pay $150k, and everything between. I applied to real estate jobs, sports-related jobs, computer jobs, writing jobs, and more. I just needed a job that would pay more than my unemployment checks (not hard to achieve) and then I'd work out what I wanted to do with my life from there. Anything that seemed remotely enjoyable, achievable, or profitable besides customer service got my resume. I couldn't admit it to myself that that is probably where I was now most employable.

I applied 255 times in a three-month span. Within those 90 days, the results were shocking. My super-impressive, optimistically sent resume was put to the test, and guess how many job offers it led to? That's right, absolutely none. And how many interviews did it lead to? None. How many e-mail replies did it get? None. While we are at it, I also received nary a networking opportunity, call-back, or referral. It led to nothing. Nil, nought, nix. Okay, I got 77 generic, "We received your resume and will contact you if we see a fit," automatic robot e-mails. Each one ended with, "Do not reply to this e-mail." Screw you too, robot.

Whaaat??? I had applied to more than 250 jobs and did not receive any contact from any human life form. Machines had crushed my dreams—which is not fair, because they have no feelings to hurt back. What was going wrong here? It worked last time, when I was a sour puss. Why is it backfiring when I'm an optimist?!

Did all of corporate America get taken over by robots? Is the economy really that bad? There are indeed job listings, so it's not that they aren't hiring. My resume was triple checked for spelling and grammar mistakes. All clear. I checked online and my book was still up there getting rave reviews. I Googled myself: nothing too offensive found.

Then I figured it out. I was getting lost in the resume database system! Duh. No one was actually reading my resume, and if no one reads it, then no one is going to contact me about it. Of course, how can anybody find me with tens of thousands of people applying for the same jobs? The squeaky wheel gets the greased palm, right?

So I decided to change that. I took the top 10 jobs I wanted the most and wrote each a cover letter tailored specifically for each one. My letter made it clear that I had researched the company and explained how I knew it was a good fit for me. I completely devoured the job listing and addressed how my skills correlated to each requirement. Not only that, I sent my cover letter and resume directly to the hiring person mentioned in the job listing. And I didn't just send it by e-mail; I sent it by FedEx. Also included in the envelope was a signed copy of my first book (a collector's item worth precisely the retail price of my book). Straight to the front of the line I go!

Subversive Job Tip

If you know the decision maker at the company who can get you a job, then you are ahead of the game. Check the press releases to learn the format of the company's e-mail addresses. The marketing department always puts a contact name and e-mail address on there for journalists to follow-up with. With this information, you can now directly e-mail anyone in the company. But don't blast a resume, e-mail a value-add instead. Find an article online, specifically a trend piece or creative way of doing business that applies directly to this person and his or her company and send it over in an e-mail. Say "I don't believe we have met, but I read this online and I thought you might find it interesting for you and your company. It's about what company X is doing with Y." And then in your signature put your name and LinkedIn profile or Website. Don't even ask about a job. Do this about every three weeks, even if you don't get a reply. Eventually, you'll start to build a rapport and after a few months send an invite to a local networking event or to a lunch meet-up to discuss how you think you can help the company. Bonus points: Use SpyPig.com or WhoReadMe.com to track how often your e-mails get read and forwarded.

Subversive evil genius was at work, and I was finally going to get noticed. I looked around for a monocle but had to improvise with a glass coaster. And if I could have gotten my cat to sit in my lap for more than three seconds, I would have petted him. I didn't care that I was in my house by myself channeling Dr. Evil to an audience of none. Soon I would have my own pool of laser sharks. My creativity was finally going to get me a job I coveted. I did it by thinking outside of the box— which was also a required skill mentioned in the job listing. My reliance on government aid would be no more!

But there was one problem with this approach. My replies were null. *Again.*

Man, it hurts when evil genius fails, especially in my delicate financial situation. I needed to find a job like never before, and I just spent $72.58 I didn't have FedExing big-wigs with nothing to show for it. Not only couldn't I get an interview, I couldn't even get someone to talk to me—my wife included. I had to pinpoint what I was doing wrong, as I knew I was a good hire. I definitely had skills, I previously got great reviews when I worked a day job, and I had indeed accomplished more than most. My skills were still relevant; my resume clearly highlighted that I had just improved customer support by 4 percentage points in 3 months! Why wasn't I piquing the interest of those hiring? I knew I was worthy, even if I had a bit of fake confidence getting me to that mindset. Why didn't anyone with an open position think so? I had to get to the bottom of this, and quickly. This was a riddle I had to solve before my entire life financially and emotionally imploded. Depression would creep back soon and ruin everything again.

So the first thing I did was decide to put myself in the hiring person's shoes. If I was a hiring manager, what would be my job motivation? Like every employee in any department, two elements would probably be job satisfaction and job security. Both of these things for me would come from creating a track record of great hires: people who have excelled at roles, people who have had longevity at the company, people who made everyone's lives easier around them. If I did this, I would probably make everyone in the office happier. They would look fondly at me and say, "Well done! You deserve a raise!" That probably happens constantly in HR offices around the world, right, guys?

Okay, let's be real. Most likely no one would notice. If I were in the HR department, then hiring qualified applicants is what would be expected of me. Plus, everyone not in my position would probably think it is the easiest task in the world because they've never had to do it. People would expect me to bring in great hires for every job opening, and if somebody didn't work out, then I'd finally get noticed and not in a good way. My ass would be on the line. Each bad seed I brought onboard would put me in the hot seat at work, and my job security would be out the door like the person just fired.

I'd have to answer for Slow Moving Sam who unexpectedly needed eight weeks of training and Flighty Flora who suddenly quit with no notice after four months on the job—and also explain why everyone I hired had alliterative nicknames.

I figured if I were a hiring manager, people would only notice me if I hired poorly. Along with probably 40 other things I had to get done in a day, having to deal with explaining to my whole office why I hired some sap who screwed everyone over would just be a big pain in the neck, not to mention a big blemish on my annual review. As a hiring manager, my new responsibility moving forward would be CMA (cover my ass).

At that point, I would CMA by only hiring highly skilled, highly experienced, or highly recommended individuals. If I could document a person was two or three of these things, then I would be protected. I would have documented proof supporting that Experienced Ethan or Educated Elaine was a good hire. It wouldn't be my fault if it didn't work out. I had a safety net as I could prove they were vetted somehow. With low-risk hires, my job would remain secure.

These may have been sweeping statements, but I had nothing to go on at the time, and I was getting desperate. Of course, higher-ups will come through occasionally and disrupt things in HR by demanding to "hire someone as fast as possible," "find someone who will work for less," or "hire my girlfriend's daughter now." (As a true pro, I would still CMA via getting these instructions documented in an e-mail.) But by figuring this out, it became my new frame of mind: most likely a hiring person in the corporate world is either someone looking for the perfect fit (time-permitting) or someone looking for the least risky choice.

To have the best chances at getting hired, I concluded it's best to be both. A quick self-analysis found that my resume goes against both these main characteristics: I wasn't the perfect hire, and I was really high risk.

I wasn't the perfect fit because my experience was all over the map. By listing all my entrepreneurial ventures on my resume, it appeared I switched jobs (really, careers) often. I'd been in the tech, customer service, real estate, finance, food and beverage, television, and publishing industries during a span of 10 years. I definitely knew a little about a lot, but not a lot about any one thing (specifically, lacking expertise in the main points of the job). My formal education did not match my profession in many cases (any job I was applying for that was non-tech related). And my job had taken the most peculiar career progression as I jumped back and forth between junior-level corporate gigs and being the CEO of my own entrepreneurial projects.

I was risky because my hobbies and interests, such as owning bars and writing books, seemed like distractions to any potential full-time gig. My entrepreneurial success said little about how I would be able to operate in a corporate environment, mainly, could I handle not being the boss? And the dynamics of a millionaire working under someone potentially much less financially secure (my resume obviously omitted my current financial desperation) is probably not worth exploring for many corporate cultures.

So in short, my resume may have been impressive to me, but it had red flags and wildcards all over it when held in the hands of an HR professional. A jack-of-all-trades read clearly as a bad hire, so I had to make wholesale changes to it if I ever wanted to get more than a robotic reply to my applications.

After learning the hard way there shouldn't be one ubiquitous resume, I created a tailor-made resume specifically for each industry I was applying for. If I was applying for a job in tech, I used my tech resume. This resume made no mention of my book, bar and restaurant experience, or television work. If it didn't directly correlate with the position I was applying for, I took it off.

If I was applying for a job in real estate, I would use my real estate resume. This one made no mention of my tech experience, but did mention my commercial and residential real estate experience, but still no book mention. If I was applying for a writing gig, then yes, finally I'd use my credentials of being a published author to my advantage.

And then you know what started happening? After two weeks of this new format, I started getting replies. Some led to introductions to other companies that had a short-term contract. Some just led to a new face on my online business and networking page (LinkedIn.com or Facebook's Branchout), which could mean a potential job connection down the road. Some led to interviews to jobs that I didn't get. I received one opportunity at a start-up doing marketing, but it was non-paying. However, this small change, the streamlining of my resume, started opening doors to real, live, breathing human beings. What a welcome change! It also made being optimistic that much easier.

My resume no longer screamed, "hot shot who knows everything." Instead, it slightly nudged, "low-risk and well-versed industry veteran." That is because everything mentioned on it somehow directly correlated to their business, their industry, or the skill set they were looking for. My resume now had one focus with logical career progressions. In addition, my outside interests were all career-related and now complementary to the job I was applying for. But my tweaking didn't stop there.

Some resumes in my arsenal were gaining more traction than others, and some were still getting ignored no matter what I did. From this frustration, I started doing A/B testing with my resumes. A/B testing is a well-known marketing strategy where you create a baseline control (my current resume), then make one variable control (a tweak to it) and compare the results.

My one tweak would be as simple as listing my education at the bottom rather than the top, rephrasing my experience at my last job, or even just removing the title of my first book, *A Million Bucks by 30*. I would compare the results (any human contact within 10 days) after about every 20 I sent out. If I got more traction with my tweaked resume, then that became my new baseline. And then I'd do the A/B test again with a different tweak. If the results came back with fewer responses, then I would keep my baseline and tweak some other part of it during my next round.

After creating over 100 different resumes in about four different industry-specific categories, I had learned a lot. I'm not exactly sure why, but every test showed that mentioning my book was career suicide. So I stopped doing it. Maybe listing the book was too much of a distraction, or it overshadowed my industry-specific work. Maybe people just hated the bragging, egotistical title (nah, that couldn't have been it).

If I really wanted to get a $100,000 salary quickly, I figured I should focus on the industry where my resume was getting the most attention: technology. I knew the customer service positions were available for me, but I wanted out of that line of work. It made sense that tech was also getting positive reactions, as it was the one industry where I had the most experience and education. Those in writing, real estate, and television were put to the side. If I wanted that to be my career, I would have to put more effort into building and expanding on my qualifications. I could go back to school, earn certifications, or attend conferences to ramp up my education and begin networking. I could also freelance, volunteer, create my own company, or even intern for experience. For now, I didn't have time for any of those things. I had pinpointed my most fitting industry (or the one most accepting of me), and now I just had to figure out what specific job within that field was perfect for me. I felt somehow, someway, I had a six-figure salary waiting for me within technology. I just wasn't sure where. And I was still unsure how I was going to do it, when I'd get there, or if I would even like it. I just had to find any job first, and then work my way up the ladder from there and figure it out as I went. My blind optimism was at doing one thing really well; it was keeping me moving forward. I wasn't going to get paid anything for sending out resumes, but I felt like I was getting closer to finding something. Yes, just a simple change in mindset helped me get there.

Subversive Job Search 101

Your resume is your business card, your elevator pitch, and your brand all in one. It's speaking for you, representing you, and stereotyping you to others in a matter of seconds. It needs to be extremely focused, constantly groomed, and field-tested often. The feedback you get, when accessed honestly, can earn you great dividends. The more time you put into it, the more you learn and the more the resume does the work for you.

An optimistic attitude allows you to overcome obstacles, think creatively, and accept challenges. Just thinking "I'm the best" made the job hunt even better. It got my brain juices flowing and thinking "How can I get them to notice me?" Although my sly attempts at cutting to the front of the hiring line at first failed, it eventually led me to A/B testing my resume to get results. My newfound positive thinking mindset led to asking "Why don't they see how awesome I am?" instead of getting frustrated by the lack of replies and blindly believing "they all think I'm a worthless hire."

In the end, people want to hire dependable, educated, and low-risk employees. Training is expensive, so get trained first. Education is important, so prove you know the subject matter through blog writing, conference attendances, or earning industry-based or task-based certifications. And lastly, don't get discouraged when your resume gets completely ignored. It just means a tweak is probably in order: you just aren't *appearing* as the "right fit" yet.

This might sound silly, but I think everyone should have at least five resumes minimum. If the most impressive thing on your resume is your college degree, then put education at the top. If your most impressive thing is experience, then put your experience at the top. And if your most impressive thing is your skill set, then put a skills box at the top. If you have nothing that is more impressive than the rest like I did, then it's crucial to A/B test the hell out of it. Something that you think is impressive sounding on your resume just might be the one thing that is creating a negative reaction. In the end, it's working smarter over working harder. A perfectly tailored resume travels much farther than a resume that tries to fit all possible jobs out there.

The best way to get hired at your target job or profession is to improve the chances of get-

What You Can Do Today

ting found. To enhance search engines finding your resume, it is super important to identify what people may be searching to find a new hire. The way it works is similar to how Google works. If you type in a certain phrase or keyword in your search terms, it will return results matching with those keywords.

So think about how people may search for your resume(s) on a job listing site such as Monster.com, Yahoo Jobs, or even within a company's own internal resume database. With this knowledge, it's best to put key phrases and industry terms on your resume, especially the name of the vertical you worked in or worked with. For example, a sales person is stopping short by putting this: "My clients were NBC, ABC, and CBS." Instead I would rephrase it: "As a media-focused sales rep, I worked with television clients NBC, ABC, and CBS."

With the second phrasing, anyone searching *media sales*, *television rep*, or *media clients* would find you along with those searching for experience at a specific network.

You've just tripled your chances of being found. Adding as many phrases or skills you expect others to search for is the key to being discovered. With this in mind, I recommend putting a skills box on your resume to list any unique or highly coveted skills you may have too. You are never sure what keyword people may type in to discover your resume. Obviously don't go overboard and appear desperate. I'd say keep to 25 skills maximum in your skills box, and try to include the most in-demand and recent technical skills you have required. Generic skills such as "hard-working" and "quick learner" are rarely searched by a hiring manager, plus they are so ubiquitous on resumes that they have become meaningless. It's more likely someone will search for a working knowledge of programs such as Photoshop, Excel, or SQL. You don't necessarily have to have mastered these skills, but you must be familiar with them and be able to talk about how you have applied them in either a workplace environment or personal project.

On another note, if you have experience starting your own business or even freelancing as a one-person company, you can call yourself a CEO. However, do not put CEO as your title anywhere on your resume unless you are applying for another CEO job. It's off-putting, because nobody wants to hire someone going backward in his or her career. Instead, give yourself a similar title (not the exact same) at your start-up as the one you are applying for, and list all your responsibilities within your one-man shop that apply solely to this title. Once you get called into the interview, you can then reveal you ran the whole company and state, "But this one part of it was what I enjoyed and did the best, which is why I'm looking to make it my career."

If you are looking to work for your dream job or your dream company, there are a few backdoors to getting hired. Call its front desk and ask if they have a current temporary employment agency they use. If so, contact this temp agency and provide it your resume specifically tailored for your dream company's line of work. If you can get your foot in the door at your dream company through its temp agency, it's a great way to get noticed. If you can prove yourself as a solid temp employee, there just may be room for you to be hired full-time.

I also recommend you taking some excellent advice from Charlie Hoehn. Being frustrated with his lack of job prospects in a sluggish economy, the recent college grad contacted his mentors and offered to work for free. His online slideshow[i] on working for free is well traveled around the Internet and worth checking out. When doing free work, there is no commitment on either party, so worst-case scenario, you can get constructive criticism of your work while increasing your work resume or portfolio. The chances are your work will be of high quality (because you busted your ass) and then you offer to work for free again. And again. It eventually becomes a profitable venture because they will a) either begin to need you and demand more work and thus offer you a job, or b) provide referrals to other top-tier companies that can pay you now.

The former CEO I worked for who hated my customer service skills shared a story about why he (supposedly) was going to approve my retroactive salary. When he was younger he worked in a grocery store, and his first two weeks on the job he demanded not to get paid. He refused to talk payment with the manager until after working there two weeks voluntarily. Those first two weeks he busted ass and was the hardest working employee they have ever seen. He made sure the grocery store manager would miss having him if he ever decided to leave. He made sure he made everyone's life around him easier, going above and beyond his actual duties, and also getting it all done with a smile on his face. Of course this move paid off well for him. During the pay rate discussion at the beginning of the third week, his offered hourly pay was more than everyone else's in the store. He effectively got a substantial raise after two weeks of upfront hard work instead of after a year's worth of hard work. This is a great tactic that could benefit many new hires willing to work hard and work for free. The pay off will be worth it in more ways than one.

Salary Science

If you spend enough time with recruiters or in the office of an employment agency, you'll eventually come across a heuristic that 70 percent of job-hunting success is based on packaging and marketing skills. This of course leaves the remaining 30 percent of job-hunting success based on the candidate's actual qualifications. Although I couldn't find the actual data supporting this statement, it doesn't mean there isn't some truth to it.

Using eye-tracking software on its Website during a 10-week period, the job-listings site The Ladders[2] (which only has six-figure job listings) found that recruiters spent an average of just six seconds looking at a resume. That's right, your entire life's work is judged the in the same amount of time as the average male orgasm. If you are unfamiliar with that reference, six seconds is also the average length of time of a non-storm ocean wave, the maximum length of time etiquette experts recommend for a hug, the amount of time an attack move lasts in the game World of Warcraft, and it's the average lifespan of a play in volleyball. People stay on bulls longer. (If you don't get any of those references, then you possibly have bigger issues than what I can help you with in garnering a better job with a higher salary.)

In short, recruiters and hiring managers don't read your resume, they scan it. And they usually scan it in formation of a capital F. The Ladders study shows they spend 80 percent of their time looking at these main items:

- Name
- Current title/company
- Previous title/company
- Previous position start and end dates
- Current position start and end dates
- Education

After six seconds a recruiter will slot your resume as either a fit or not and move on. To make those six seconds count the most, The Ladders recommend not using distractions such as photos or graphs, have bullet points rather than paragraphs, and if possible, use a professionally-written resume service to make it easier for them to scan for necessary information as fast as possible.

A survey[3] of HR managers by author Susan Britton Whitcomb found 67 percent of respondents felt that the length of a resume should be one to two pages long, with only 21 percent saying it needed to be "as long as needed to convey the applicant's qualifications." I'm in agreement with the future-thinkers from the Career Thought Leaders Consortium[4] who think the future in resumes will be the 140 character limit of Twitter posts. With this route, you could Tweet a company your most basic or most important skills for a quick two-sentence introduction. This will allow you to show (and not waste precious characters saying it) that you "get" social media and that you are technology savvy, both great credentials in most careers. Not every company has a Twitter account, but for those who do, this might be a good way to get your foot in the door and get noticed.

This same consortium also predicts a rising trend of mini-resumes. This is basically a condensed resume on your business card or an entire resume on a business card that can unfurl all your accomplishments to the reader if desired. This is a great networking tool when you want to slip someone your card but not shove your elevator pitch down his throat upon first contact. Check out ResuMiniMe.com and PrintingForLess.com/Mini-Resume.html for some ideas.

I firmly believe that everyone should have an online presence. Just a paper resume makes you irrelevant. You can create a decent Website for less than $50 or use free business social programs such as LinkedIn. Someone will most likely Google your name prior to hiring you, and you should do all you can to control what they find. If what they find is positive and it reaffirms what they already know about you, you begin appearing as the low-risk and worthy hire you need to be.

3

Career Test Drive

I have negative funds in my bank account. I can't even afford something that is free, that's more than I have. I have to raise 10 bucks just to be broke.

—Louis C.K.

Seeing that the tech sector was a bright possibility and gaining some traction for me in my subversive job search, I took a moment to reflect. I wanted to take my career by the balls and be the one in charge, but I was feeling like my career choice had me by the balls—which if you've not been made aware, is painful. I wasn't in love with tech support; it was just something I had a lot of experience in. I had the most experience in it only because it was my first job ever. It reminded me how, at one point, I couldn't get a job because I didn't have any experience. But of course, I didn't have any experience because I couldn't get a job. It's a frustrating loop to be in, but at least my loop was now paying me for my frustration. For me, the grass always seemed greener in the other departments. Although tech was the most promising, I needed to shake this feeling that I was settling and try to venture into something different.

In addition to having the time to take yoga classes multiple times a day, being unemployed offered one thing: flexibility. Because I was hopelessly unemployed with no options, now was the time for me to try something brand new and test the waters in a few different industries that always enticed me. If I didn't do it now, I knew I would always feel stuck in tech. I didn't just want to subversively work my way up to a $100,000 salary; I also wanted to be happy knowing I did it in a field I selected.

I always heard that if I did something I loved, money would just come naturally. Most of the people I knew were either doing something they were passionate about or they were making six-figures. It was always mutually exclusive. I hoped to be the rare dude that could pull off this even rarer double rainbow and get paid handsomely for doing something I loved. So I gave myself one month to find a new career direction. If after a month with no success, then I'd focus back on the tech sector, knowing I gave it my all in trying a new career move.

With my four week deadline set, I narrowed my focus to two verticals that I knew I would love working in: real estate and sports. If I was going to go full-on corporate, it might as well be within an industry that I read about daily.

Because I could always finagle myself into a newspaper, periodical, or TV show using various free methods that I highlighted in my first book, I anticipated my skills would transfer nicely to marketing and public relations. So after identifying this niche target, I tailored four different resumes for my four future "passionate" careers: sports marketing, sports public relations, real estate marketing, and real estate public relations. Doing something that was an interest of mine seemed the best way to be able to eventually reach my pie-in-sky salary target. Also, I knew some changes in my job-hunting behavior were in order. Because my goal was to receive a job offer in either the sports or real estate industries within the next four weeks, I committed to spending at least one hour a day sending resumes to qualified listings. Each application would come with a cover letter and a tailored resume to match. I also made a commitment to spend at least an hour identifying and improving any shortcomings of making me a qualified candidate within these fields. I would do this comparing career progressions outlined on LinkedIn of people whose position I wanted, scouring job listings looking for repetitive skill set criteria, and reading as much as I could about the industry. I now had actionable items that would help me reach my goal, which made the job hunt a little more structured.

Instead of resume-bombing entry-level careers within these fields, I started resume-sniping. I found listings and created a laser-guided resume to match for each listing. I spent additional time reviewing other people's online resumes in these fields to see where I needed to make up ground. I researched industry conferences, seminars, and more, to see what I could do to improve my credentials and begin networking. Because I had previously learned so much by A/B testing my resume, I used similar tactics with my new sniping efforts. I got a reply two weeks in for a marketing position at a real estate start-up. One catch: it had no pay. Of course, no pay doesn't sound much like a job, right? It sounds more like an internship—or maybe indentured servitude. I always thought jobs meant there was some sort of compensation. Further digging revealed there were indeed reparations in exchange for labor, but it was earned equity in the company each month you worked there. As majority of start-ups fail, these shares are usually worthless currency. On the other hand, pre-funded start-ups like this one had nothing else to offer as they usually aren't actually cash-flow positive until several years down the road (if they are even still around then). It should be noted, that being employed in a start-up often comes with expectations to work 60 to 80 hours a week. On the positive side, if you are working at a start-up, it's probably a cutting-edge technology created by a bunch of intelligent people looking to change the world. That kind of environment is inspiring, fun, and educational. Due to this, and the miniscule workforce of most start-up communities within each city, networking and connecting with other hot shots and industry-leaders comes naturally. Start-up founders and employees instantly become each other's cheerleaders, building a really gratifying support network—maybe because you may need each other in case your current company ends up collapsing and you have to find a new gig quickly. The thing that keeps everyone going is that there is a chance, albeit small chance, that they'll be an "instant" millionaire 10 years down the road when the company becomes the next hot thing. This environment of high risk, high reward is not for everyone, especially for someone ideally looking to make a $100,000 salary as quick as possible in order to support a family. It was ludicrous for me to even entertain the job offer with no salary, and even knowing that, I took the non-paying job.

I took it for a few reasons. I didn't want to return back to being in a rut. I found I needed a reason to shower, shave, and dress each day—basic hygiene does not come naturally for me. Additionally, it didn't automatically discount me from collecting my unemployment checks, which were becoming a more and more important part of my week. I could save my job-hunting for nights, time permitting. But the main factor for accepting the job was simple: it fit squarely within the defined goal that I set up for myself. The company was real-estate related—a Website that helped discover new neighborhoods—and the position was to control all their marketing efforts. I had achieved my stated goal in the stated timeframe and in my eyes, this offer was a reason to celebrate! It happened all very quickly and felt like the right move. Yes, it lacked a salary, but I was already willing to start at the bottom and work my way up just to see where it took me. My plan was to first go after the industry, then go after the money. I reasoned that this new start-up experience could be a valuable asset that pays for itself in any future position I may have.

I devoured book after book on marketing theory, marketing trends, and marketing ideas. I loved reading about these ideas, and I was ready to put them in practice. And I went to work. It just felt good to get on the subway, go to an office, and be productive again. In between absorbing the new industry terms and technologies and meeting potential partners, I helped run online marketing campaigns, garnered some press mentions, and arranged a conference exhibit. But three months into the job, I identified a few important things about being at this start-up: I loved the people, I loved the product, and I loved the environment. I also loved learning something new. But the one negative that kept gnawing at me was that I just loathed actually doing the marketing work. Well, I loved the principles of it: I liked how being creative can get a customer excited about your product, I liked building brands, and I liked meeting and learning what customers wanted. But I just didn't like executing it. It just wasn't satisfying for me and I never felt done. No matter what, there is always more marketing to do. Of course endless work is the expectation of a start-up employee's life, but I wasn't finding it as rewarding as I had anticipated. So in the end it took me three months to figure out that marketing was not meant to be my career, and I was okay with that. It was a personality thing between me and the occupation, and I was learning something about myself. I considered it a win. By learning what I hated as a career, it brought me closer to finding something I loved.

I didn't have another three months to test drive a new career though. It also took these first 90 days for it to really hit me that a real paycheck at this start-up, no matter what amount, would realistically not occur for at least a couple more years. Telling my wife this, I could start to feel her unquestioning support beginning to wane. I couldn't blame her, for the past 12 months she had single-handedly kept our family afloat with a steady paycheck from her job. Without her, we would have no doubt been bankrupt and possibly homeless. It was time to get my shit together, to stop screwing around with trying on new careers, and to start earning a freaking paycheck again. My wife supported that idea, though "supported" may be a weak word for it.

I went to resume-sniping at night while keeping my commitments to my non-paying marketing job during the day. Sleep could wait. I had no regrets for my three-month sojourn into the unknown world of marketing. I was proud of myself for going after what I wanted; I would have regretted it if I hadn't. However, I was not proud of my bank balance or lack of foresight into what I was getting into by accepting a no-pay job. Once we were financially secure, then maybe I could experiment again. So I sat down and was really honest with myself. I had to accept that if I ever wanted to earn $100,000 in the near future, it probably had to get done in technology. There had to be a role I could master, maybe even enjoy, within the tech sector. I felt I needed to give myself a deadline this time to make this dream a reality, because I find I work best under deadlines, as they keep me focused, on task, and able to easily evaluate my progress. To remind myself daily of my goal, I changed the text of my phone's alarm clock. So now, every morning at 7:05 a.m., when my phone's alarm goes off, I would be forced to read "You will have a $100,000 technology career soon." This daily morning reminder kept my goal fresh in my head.

Because I was getting a little more desperate, I took another step in the take-this-a-little-more-seriously direction and started honing my resume-sniping skills with A/B testing my cover letters as well. Of course, the results increased a little bit more too. (The recurring theme here in most of my life-lessons is basically that being indolent doesn't work.)

After a month, I got an e-mailed reply from another small company, albeit this one had been around 10 years and was cash-flow positive. They had the luxury of providing pay checks. The reply was just one sentence long, and it contained the most loaded question possible:

Alan, what are your salary requirements?

—Don

Whoa! I was ecstatic a human e-mailed me, but how was I going to respond to this Pandora's Box of an opening line? My response would really determine how the rest of the conversation would play out. I didn't want to just go for the $100,000 goal, as I'd probably price myself out and it would be the end of the conversation. But if I undersold myself, I'd be working for less than I should or come off as too green, and not worth their time.

I Googled the company (then Binged it just to be sure), searched their job listings online, and tried to remember what job I actually applied for that generated this response. I also had to determine what the company actually did. Their vague Website was not too helpful. It did have some open jobs listed on it, though they seemed to be for entry-level jobs only. I was okay taking an entry-level job, but not back in the tech industry where I had accumulated nine years experience. That should be worth something. Entry-level would be understandable in a new occupation, and this listing seemed to be working again at a computer help desk, similar to the one I retired from a year before. It was also a marketing software company, and that I had recent marketing experience is probably why I looked like a potential fit. (Note to self: working for free at that start-up paid off after all.)

I'd never had a job that paid more than $55,000, so I debated how I should reply back to Don, the man with no time for a last name. I couldn't be too picky because this was a ripe opportunity to get a paying gig, but on the other hand, I wanted this to be as lucrative as possible. One thing I've learned is that most negotiations are all about confidence. Whoever has the most confidence usually comes out ahead, whether that confidence is faked or not. I definitely was not in a confident position; I had never been so anxious in my life for a paying job. I couldn't even comprehend what would happen once my unemployment checks ran out.

I sat at my keyboard terrified. I had no choice but to drop to my knees and pray to Buck Greenback and the Legal Tenders, my imaginary money god and his disciples in the sky. (Although they are often mistaken for an oldies cover band, they play mostly originals, some Pink Floyd.) The cosmic feedback I got was to approach my reply by first addressing Don by his first name rather than figuring out his last name and calling him "Mr." The first name route would make me appear as an equal, and not someone instantly beneath him. Then my spiritual advisors counseled me to type in a slightly far-reaching salary, but to give Don an out just in case I scared him away with my big number. Then they suggested I should end it with some skills that were not on my resume, but that I learned were complementary to the position based on my online research of the company. I couldn't think of anything better, so I went with Buck and the band on this one.

So I wrote:

Thanks for getting back to me, Don. Salary is negotiable, as I'm more in the hunt to look for the "right fit." That said, ideally $70,000+ would be the range. Please let me know if that's something that would work for you.

I should mention that along with my tech support experience, I also have a marketing and content management background that could assist in additional roles.

Regards,

Alan Corey

And then I checked my e-mail every 45 seconds for the next two days. I was convinced I aimed too high. I was also itching to get back to a regular paycheck and was second-guessing my far-reaching number. But as soon as I was about to give up and chalk this up to being too greedy, Don wrote me back:

That's way outside our budget for this particular position; however, we may have something else to consider you for. Let me get back. Thanks.

I instantly started taking Buck Greenback's name in vain and ripping the Legal Tenders a new one. I had shot myself in the foot and played this all wrong! Regaining my composure a few minutes later, I reread his e-mail and noticed there was still some bait left on this fishing hook. I wanted this to be a big catch, so I wrote back quickly, "Thanks, Don—I hope to hear from you soon." Short and sweet. Any backpedalling to a lower number at this point would just make me look like a pathetic, desperate, and wavering employee, the exact opposite of anything anyone would want to hire regardless of the salary. I committed to $70,000 as my number at the beginning of the e-mail chain, and all my actions had to match this amount of money moving forward. Also in my head I had to believe I was worth $70,000, even at a time when a paycheck of any amount would be a welcome improvement. If I didn't believe I was worth $15,000 more than I have ever made before, then no one would believe it, even in an e-mail correspondence.

My worrying was short-lived, because my strategy worked! A few days later Don called me in to be interviewed for an unlisted position for an Application Manager. I wasn't sure what that title meant, but during the interview I found out it was a mix of project management and sales. I felt like I had limited experience in both, but I didn't tell him that. Instead, I talked at length what I've done in those fields. When asked about my one-year customer service experience, I didn't bad mouth the previous employer one bit. And I definitely didn't mention my nasty bonus-losing firing. I put a healthy spin on things and I said I outgrew the position that I was hired for and took on added responsibilities throughout the year. I informed him that I left because they were unable to pay me what I was looking for. It's true and paints a rosy picture of me as a hard-working employee, instead of one that comes with a firing and a lot of question marks. It went as perfect as an interview could go. On the spot I got offered the job, and conveniently enough, the salary they offered was exactly $70,000. (Maybe I should have asked for more?) I accepted, shook hands with Don, exited the office, and silently asked for forgiveness to my spiritual rock band in the sky, which was currently jamming The O'Jays "For the Love of Money."

Round up a couple un-employed buddies of similar interests and create a resume

Subversive Job Tip

lemonade stand/car wash/bake sale/dog-walking service/lawn-mowing service. Set up a table outside the headquarters of the company you want to work or in a well-populated business district or park, and offer a free service or product (make it top-notch) in exchange for taking a resume. For ease, have your condensed resume and those of all your friends combined on a double-sided paper for easy take-away, along with headshot and LinkedIn urls. Stand-up and greet passers-by with a smile, offering your free product and resume. Repeat your length of time: "We'll be here every Monday and Friday for this month only," or "We'll be here everyday this week." This creates familiarity as you get to see repeat customers, and they now know they have to take action quickly before your defined end date arrives. That your service or product is free should also be heavily accentuated. If you notice a repeat customer, ask if you can get his or her business card to talk about how you'd like to do more than run a lemonade stand, bake sale, or car wash. Bonus Points: Print your resume on napkins or paper cups so they are forced to take it with them. If they insist on giving you something in return, ask for payment in written recommendations on LinkedIn about your creative hustle.

I gave my notice to the start-up that my marketing days were coming to an end and started my new paying gig four weeks later. I was thrown in the fire and noticed a lot of things about my job that I wasn't expecting. Along with project management and sales, I was also a client manager. I was the point of contact for a list of clients and I had to always make them happy. They'd call me if their software wasn't working right, or if they wanted to add new features to it, or if they wanted to know when the latest upgrade was coming in. On the other hand, I also had to quote, plan, budget, manage, and test every version of their software creation and implementation. In my role at this software business, I was really going to be product manager, project manager, quality assurance manager, customer service, tech support, and client manager all in one. But my title was just "Application Manager." Oh, the joys of working in a start-up. You wear many hats because there aren't very many heads.

Working these many different roles allowed me to test drive many different careers within technology all at once. I learned quickly that sales wasn't my bag. I found myself excelling at quality assurance (finding bugs in the software), but it wasn't something I necessarily enjoyed—the same with customer service and tech support. However, product management allowed me to be creative and come up with new features for the software, which was fun and interesting to do. Likewise, project management, making sure the project came in on time and on budget, was something I found rewarding. It also reminded me of the additional responsibilities I had assigned to me at the electronics dealer when I was bargaining for a retroactive salary. Project and product management both felt like something that came as a natural fit for me, and I took a mental note that maybe one of these would be my career direction one day.

It took me three months to get in a headspace of really finding out the ins and outs of my newest job among the different hats I wore. Like any job, it had its pros and cons, and I started anticipating my next steps on how to generate a bigger salary from it. I definitely would have to get creative in order to get a raise just three months in. It was time to be subversive once again.

Subversive Job Search 101

If trying new industries and new occupations interests you, by all means go for it. It may mean entry-level only positions, which is respectable. Happiness should always be your first motivating factor. I tried marketing, grasped quickly it wasn't as rosy as I'd anticipated, and then went back to where I was comfortable, working with software. But working for free in a new industry did open up doors for me in my next job search. I would definitely do it again in a heartbeat.

When job hunting, you really do get back what you put in to it. The more time I spent crafting a cover letter, and the more I tweaked and tailored the resume, the more responses I got back. Instead of blindly throwing darts at a moving target, I started targeting and focusing on strategic matches. It's crucial to spend a good portion of your cover letter talking about how you anticipate helping the company and provide concrete examples. If you are just talking about yourself in your cover letter, then it appears you haven't done much research on the company. Address the person by name in the cover letter that you anticipate you will be working for. "To whom it may concern" also calls into question your research skills. If you come across a company you like, but they don't have your job listed, don't be afraid to apply anyway. You never know, they may be hiring for another role that isn't posted yet or they may earmark your resume and file it in their "potential future hire" bin. I have a friend who has gotten plenty of interviews by e-mailing the CEO of a company directly, completely bypassing having to look for job-postings. It has a low percentage rate, but when it works, he's already got an in with the most influential person in the company, and that obviously goes a long way. Unless specified in the job listing not to, a follow-up phone call a few days after you apply is always highly recommended. This simple act ensures they at least know your name and will most likely take the time to look at your resume. You already have a step up on all the other applicants.

It's important to start a job hunt with a salary number you are committed to. This helps frame your mindset in your e-mails, phone conversations, and interviews. I had set my number at $70,000, and I just kept asking myself questions like "What would a person making $70,000 say right here? How would a person making $70,000 reply to this e-mail? What does a person making $70,000 dress like?" After doing this constant check-in before all your workplace conversations and transactions, it will start coming naturally to you. And then you move up your salary mark to $80,000 and repeat.

Luckily, I got back an offer of $70,000 to the non-posted position at the new technology company. It didn't have a bonus, just straight up $70,000. However, I was prepared to come back with replies if the salary came in lower. (I had already set the stage for my expected payday, so it wouldn't have been a complete surprise to them if I ended up asking for more.) If Don had offered me $60,000, I would have replied "Thank you for your offer. I'm looking for a total package of at least $70,000. What would I need to do in this position to earn a $10,000 bonus by the end of the year?" Or "If I accepted, would it be possible to have a three-month salary review? I believe I'll be able to prove I'm worth more than that to you." Then I'd make sure these things are in writing when I signed the dotted line.

Finding out what you hate is just one step closer to finding out what you love. A job with many hats can help you figure out quickly and easily what you want to pursue as a career. Maybe it's something you become passionate about, or maybe it's just something you find that you excel at. Either of these are good career criteria and potentially lucrative paths to follow.

It's always beneficial to get an idea of what your expected salary is going to be before you

What You Can Do Today

apply or interview for a new position (or even ask for a raise at your current position.) You should have a realistic number in your head of your market worth at all times. The Websites Salary.com, Payscale.com, GetRaised.com, and Glassdoor.com can give you a peek at what you are up against pay wise for similar jobs within your city. From there, you can research job listings with the same job title and descriptions to access your current value on the marketplace.

If you are new to the workforce, then you probably know exactly where you stand: at the bottom. But don't fret; focusing on entry-level careers or internships is a great strategy when just starting out. Everyone's been there at one point, and it is a numbers game, so you'll have to apply to a lot of jobs. The Website OneDayOneJob.com is a great resource for just this. You can get daily e-mails about both entry-level jobs and internships in your area or just browse their job-listing site by company, location, or field of work.

The most frustrating obstacle when applying en masse is that a company's online form will prompt you to upload your resume, and then on the next screen, you're prompted to fill out all the input boxes with the exact same information that is already in your resume! Instead of closing out the application form because of the company's idiotic redundancy, download a free app to do it for you. LastPass and RoboForm are both two-in-one applications that remembers all your passwords and automatically logs you in to all your job-hunting sites (and non-job-hunting sites too) and also has an automatic form filler function where it will pre-populate all the application forms for you. This greatly reduces your typing time and allows you to be much more productive when resume blasting in full force becomes a necessary evil. Couple one of these applications with Huntsy.com, which tracks all the jobs you have applied for and sends reminders to you for when to follow up on your applications. Now you are a well-oiled job hunting machine.

If all else fails, Trojan horse your resume into an office to get noticed. A former coworker of mine was a local food-delivery guy who would made sweet with the receptionist every day around lunch on his delivery rounds. And also with the receptionist at the company next door. And the next one. Eventually he got his resume into the hands of higher ups by a combination of asking the receptionist to pass it on and slyly sneaking it into the delivery bag. This simple act landed him a job he still works at 10 years later! If delivery is not your bag, then just add a resume with a hand-written note in every mundane task you do that involves an envelope. Stuff it in along with your check when you are paying bills or come up with a reason to write a thank-you letter to a company you have enjoyed doing business with. Okay, I know using envelopes and post offices are what old people tend to do, so at the very least add a link to your LinkedIn profile prefaced with a message of "Now Accepting Interviews" to your e-mail signature. Then write professional, viral-worthy e-mails in every correspondence, and eventually one may get forwarded to someone at the right time with the right connections, without you feeling like you've sold your soul by cramming into a wooden horse ass to get a job.

Salary Science

Experts say, when it comes to negotiating monetary terms, the rule of thumb is to let the other person throw out the first number. From there, you are in control of the rest of the negotiations. However, University of Idaho psychology professor Todd Thorsteinson's simulation experiments[1] have thrown a wrench in that. His findings show that when asking for a raise or settling on a starting salary, you should throw out the highest number possible, even laughably high, to receive the highest amount of money.

In the experiments, participants entered into a simulated job salary negotiation as either a job candidate or a hiring manager. The potential candidates previously had $29,000 yearly salaries and were now being offered a promotion. When the topic of salary came up, half the participants were instructed to jokingly request $100,000—and those who did so wound up getting 9 percent higher offers on average than those who played it straight and asked for a more reasonable raise. The average resulting offers were $35,385 versus $32,463, in favor of those asking for a huge pay increase. The findings suggest that mentioning that first high number, although unrealistic to both parties, sets a subconscious anchor in your boss's mind to compare your real salary negotiations to. Now a $10,000 raise doesn't look so absurd to your boss when he is anchoring it against your $100,000 raise request. It's akin to retailers putting an artificially high price on an item and then having a 50 percent off sale! Sure, it looks like a good sale price but really it's at the originally intended retail price.

But when asking for a raise this way, be sly about it. Being overly aggressive or attempting such a request with your boss too soon can mark you as unprofessional or unrealistic, and may backfire in an uncontrolled setting. If you are unsure where you stand, just ask for the highest reasonable salary of someone in your position based on your online research and you could come out way ahead of what you would have otherwise. When you're in doubt about what to say during a negotiation, just shut the hell up. The person listening in a negotiation is always in the power position over someone talking. If you find yourself rambling on, just stop talking. Doing this often creates an awkward moment of silence and allows you to regain the power position, as it makes the other person start talking.

Something else worth mentioning is that your body language can make or break any salary negotiation or job interview. Amy Cuddy gave an excellent TED talk[2] about how best to improve your outcome in stressful

situations with a few simple tweaks. Animals and hu-
mans are alike in that they display their statuses via
body language. High-status postures take up a lot of
space, while low-status postures take up the least. People
that have their legs spread open or hands behind their
head and leaning back are displaying their high status
to others, and if you do all three at the same time in a
power pose it can become really beneficial. High status
posing, whether consciously or subconsciously, comes
with physiological benefits. Power posing will increase
the level of your dominance hormone testosterone while
simultaneously decreasing your level of the stress hormone cortisol. This change in hormones allows you to
think more abstractly and to be more assertive, confident, and optimistic—or more accurately, be more of
yourself. It works even with just two minutes of effort.

So a secret tip before going into a tense situation
like an interview or salary discussion is to spend 120
seconds in a bathroom stall, elevator, or cubicle doing
a power pose. A Wonder Woman stance, erect with
hands on hips, is a great one. An open Jumping Jack
formation that resembles an out-stretched star would
work. Or hell, even mimicking a cowboy riding a horse
and cracking a whip can make physiological changes
in your body that will make you immediately appear
more confident, engaged, and captivating. (Unless you
are interviewing to be a power mime, do this before
the interview, not during the interview.)

Cuddy's research showed that those that chose to be hunched over looking at a phone, arms crossed and body folded, or hand on neck or face just prior to their interview were overwhelmingly given much poorer marks than those that took the time to do a power pose. And the more you do high power poses, the more you display characteristics of an effective leader, which is high dominance and low stress. Her research shows that you can actually fake it until you *become* it. So start faking it to make some serious changes.

Maintaining eye-contact and smiling is a crucial part of any bargaining agreement as it demonstrates confidence and makes the other person feel at ease. Bangor University researchers have found[3] that people prefer those who genuinely smile over those who just politely smile (genuine smiles create deeper wrinkles). Even when told that a politely smiling person will earn them more profits, those in study still preferred choosing a genuine smiler who made them less money. So those results written in a mathematic formula would be written as: Genuine > Polite > Rude > Dead.

Also, a study[4] by *Psychological Science* has found that when talking to your boss about salary numbers, don't lean to the left. People tend to underestimate values and numbers when leaning left, and you could be selling yourself short. Standing upright or leaning right equally provides more accurate number crunching and evaluation, so make sure you keep an upright posture (or a right-leaning one) when talking about your worth to others. Otherwise that extra bonus that is rightfully yours could be left to the side. Oh man, I should have left that out, right? And now all pun-haters can groan in unison.

4

Making Excellent Company

Most people work just hard enough not to get fired and get paid just enough money not to quit.

—George Carlin

I was now employed and making $70,000, so I couldn't complain. But I'm a future-thinker; I'm always envisioning what I'm going to be doing down the road. It was especially weighing on my mind as I now had eight months left to reach my $100,000 dream goal. I'd been at my new job three months, and was feeling confident in my production and value to the company. So I asked myself: "What am I working toward? How can I improve my situation? How can I make more money here in the short-term and the long-term?" Usually answers from this can be derived from also asking "How can I make this company better? How can I improve efficiency? How can I increase profit?" The better you serve the company, the better they will reward you. Well, at least the good ones do.

As an Application Manger, I had clients assigned to me, and I was responsible for serving their needs based around our software. This could be training their new hires, resolving bugs, upselling them new features and enhancements, managing the development of these add-ons, and then testing and creating documentation for these new upgrades they've ordered. My job centered on long-term relationships, as I would talk to my assigned clients almost daily. This was drastically different than the other side of the office, where the sales team sat. They were all focused on short-term relationships, and they had a commission-based contract with a strict focus on new clients. Each new client they signed on would be handed over to one of us four Application Managers to then take care of their needs for the entirety of the relationship. Then the sales team would go back to talking to potential new customers again, and we would handle everything with the newly signed client from there on out.

Now I quickly learned I had an inverse incentive for selling our company's product to my clients. The more software upgrades I sold to my assigned clients, the more I then had to product manage, project manage, QA, document, and train them on. It led to me feeling reprimanded for selling our product. This extra work would mean I would have to stay late and work the occasional weekend to meet deadlines. And then if

I couldn't sell, I would feel rewarded. Without any new projects, I would be able to finish my daily responsibilities within a reasonable time frame and leave the office by 5 p.m. Obviously this inverse incentive was not benefiting the company in any shape, way, or form.

The company had no overtime pay; we were purely salaried employees who had to find a way to get our work done, end of discussion. I figured if I could get a commission on my sales though, that it would be a win-win for the company and for me. It would now be worth the extra effort of me selling more. I had to convince upper management that this slight improvement could really improve the company's bottom line, but first I wanted to pitch the other Application Managers my plan and make sure I had their buy in. Until then, I would have no choice but to just sit at my desk and silently shit-talk my work computer's monitor. (I figured that built-in web camera meant it could read my lips.)

I met with the other three Application Managers during the course of the week, and I discussed whether they were also conflicted with sales. I wanted to make sure I wasn't misunderstanding my job's responsibilities and doing something incorrect. They confirmed I wasn't and confided in me that they weren't motivated to sell our products either. Feeling relieved that I wasn't insane, I shared my commission idea on how to make our jobs better. I didn't want to shoot ourselves in the foot somehow if this was successfully implemented. After talking through all the different angles, they couldn't find anything wrong with my proposed commission-based setup. They agreed this potential payment structure would both make them happier and make the company more profitable. Having their support, I had even more confidence to address this plan with the higher-ups.

Subversive Job Tip

Sign up for the free newsletter at HelpAReporterOut.com. You'll get a daily digest of journalists requesting interview subjects. Use this to get your name in the press for maximum exposure. If you can paint yourself an expert or a knowledgeable source, you'll more than likely become someone who gets repeat interviews. Try your best to get quoted comparing yourself to another person or company you want to be involved with or dream of working with. Once published, it offers an excellent reason for that person or company to now contact you. You must compare yourself, and not just complement the other party, otherwise the journalist will just talk about the other company and remove you from the article. Bonus Points: Set up a listing that indicates you will be writing about a specific company. With the feedback you get you can submit an unsolicited presentation to that business's marketing or HR head as a personal project you were working on to understand the company before you applied there. Sum up all the feedback on a final slide with what they are doing right, followed by suggestions for improvement.

Being a small company, we were a very flat business (many new technology companies are), so there wasn't a rigid chain of command. There were three higher-ups and then the rest of us. I decided to pitch it to them separately. The first top-level person I talked to agreed it made sense, but only wanted me to have this incentive and not any of the other Application Managers. I rejected the offer as that would have led to an instant mutiny from my co-workers. The second higher-up agreed initially and said he'd have to think about it. And the third one, Don, wanted nothing to do with it. (You remember Don, from the e-mail.)

My inspired commission pitch to improve sales, along with morale, productivity, and possibly employee retention, fell on Don's deaf ears and he convinced the remaining management team it was a bad idea too. His response was that it wasn't how he did things in his previous company, which was successful, and he didn't think we needed to do it here. Don apparently was officially calling the shots on this, so I was out of options. His brain was my brick wall. I saw no other way to improve my current salary in the short-term, even with increasing my work load by bringing the company more money. Additionally, because the corporate ladder consisted of two rungs and I was a new hire on a staff of 20, I didn't see much long-term progress sticking around and trying to get incremental promotions and bonuses. Going that route would guarantee that I would miss my $100,000 salary milestone within my pre-determined time frame. This hope for baby-step promotions was what everyone else at the company was trying to do and there weren't enough positions to go around for this to be an effective strategy. If I wanted to get a salary boost, I had to do it another way.

Every other month, the company's financial footing was a bit unstable, so maybe that's why they were hesitant to shake things up with the Application Managers pay structure. On the other hand, maybe that's exactly what they needed to do to improve the bottom line. I did the best that I could to sell them on this idea, and I know not every idea will be heard or approved, so I went about my day as I normally would, mouthing silent expletives again to my monitor. I took solace that they at least heard me out—that's better than not even giving me the time of day. I broke the bad news to the other Application Managers of my failed effort, and they grieved in their own special way of working longer days with no extra pay.

While commiserating this failed plot over lunch with my fellow Application Manager Joanna, our conversation started getting personal. We had bonded quickly, as she trained me, she also sat next to me, and we had to work together often throughout the daily schedule and reserve resources. Eventually, the highlight of each day was our lunchtime break, which turned into daily bitch and moan sessions about our job. We both felt like we were working four full-time jobs and getting paid for one. After three weeks of the same lunchtime banter, we decided to share each other's salary with each other. Now this can create a hostile situation in many cases, but she and I were very tight, and we agreed we would not take the news personally. She knew I was successful at plotting and getting bigger paychecks, and I knew she was making more than me as she was better at the job, had been there longer, and had been my trainer and mentor.

I revealed I had been making $70,000 based on the salary cap I had given myself with my first e-mail to Don. She nodded and said she expected as much. She sheepishly replied she was making $62,000 and that maybe it was because women always get paid slightly less than men. I was instantly filled with mixed emotions. On one hand, my salary cap was not a limiting factor for this job. If anything, it actually helped me to get a higher salary than what they were paying for the position. On the other hand, I didn't feel worthy as Joanna was superior skill-wise and was making far less than me. I felt bad for her, as she deserved more. Luckily, we were close friends at this point, and it didn't mean I have to worry about her poisoning my food during next lunch's bitch and moan session.

To change topics quickly, I pointed out the company had an extremely high turnover rate. It was a combination of company firings, employees quitting, and a few "we're not really sure what happened" rumors and stories of others exiting. About once a month, someone was leaving the company and a new person was coming in. That's a lot of activity for a company with just 20 employees. Maybe everyone else was seeing the light that this company was just a stepping stone to something bigger, better, and with higher pay? Or maybe the company just kept hiring low-paying individuals with the sole purpose of working them to the bone until they quit (a skeleton crew, if you will).

Joanna and I eventually discovered we both had taken our jobs out of desperation when we were hired. Not only that, it seemed to be a recurring theme with some of the other people I had talked to over other bitch and moan lunches. Sure the economy was rough, and many people were desperate for work, but this business seemed to attract them all. Or they all just liked lunching with me. My coworkers all agreed the company had uneven pay and long hours, but they were there with a job when they needed it the most. They were all appreciative of that, and were all thankful to be employed. Me included. We obviously shouldn't be grumbling. But at the same time, now having gotten a more secure footing financially, I didn't feel like it was disloyal to see others move on. It's quite possible to outgrow a company, and maybe we all had reached that point too.

Joanna and I left the table with a whole new perspective on things. We decided to research what others were making in the same role at other companies and report back what we found. I started thinking my path to a $100,000 position might take me to a different company altogether. Maybe it was time for both Joanna and I to move on. Or maybe our research would reveal we were getting paid exactly what we should be paid and that we should be enthusiastic about being employed. The results could be a wake-up call that our moaning about having a good-paying job is the most privileged bitching to have ever occurred since Veruca Salt took a tour of that chocolate factory. Either way, we had to find out where we stood among Application Managers at other companies first, and then we could decide if our entitled bitching was somewhat justified.

Nothing is more appreciated by employers than to have employees trying to figure out how

Subversive Job Search 101

to improve the company. Do research on how to improve your company's performance and if possible, try to quantify it. Numbers speak volumes. Maybe it's improving the company's hiring practices, or introducing new technology or software, or just improving a simple workflow or process. The thing is, you should make it known as much as possible that you are thinking about how to make things better. But come with well-thought-out ideas, be able to explain the benefits of that change, and make sure it will not just be benefiting you. Any boss would love it if you bring to them not just a problem, but a solution. Bonus points are earned if you take ownership of the proposed remedy. Hopefully bonuses are earned if the remedy works.

Regardless of if your ideas are ever implemented, just appreciate the fact that your company is even taking the time to listen. I would imagine any person in a significant role wouldn't mind getting an e-mail that says "Do you have 10 minutes to talk about how I think we can improve the company?" You do this enough times, and you'll start to be included in other decisions too, and being a decision-maker always improves your chances in earning promotions and raises. Also, thinking about the company makes it clear you aren't just hanging around to collect paychecks, which is most likely what everyone else is doing. Your improvement suggestions will make you stand out, be heard, and hopefully make the company do everything in their power to keep you happy and well-paid.

When thinking about your company, you should begin to take notice of internal changes, even in other departments. Training new hires is expensive and time-consuming, and can be a drain on morale. Maybe your colleagues need better training? Maybe the company needs better hiring practices? Maybe the actual position was not what was promised? Are people leaving on their own free will or are they getting fired? Are new hires seemingly underqualified and underpaid? You can use this information to help come up with other potential improvements to pitch to management. Worst case scenario, it will help you make informed decisions about the right time to think about making a career move of your own.

I find the best time for a career move for me is when I noticed I've stopped learning at work. If I'm doing the same thing now that I did six months ago, then I stop and ask myself, "Will I be doing the exact same thing six months in the future too?" If yes, then I've stopped growing and I'll probably be stuck doing this forever. I'm no longer facing new challenges or acquiring new skills. My knowledge level has peaked and I'll be stagnant from here on out. Other times a career move is in order would be if you find the business is unethical, you no longer believe in the mission of the company, you are being compensated unfairly, you are being mistreated, you are not adding value to the business, or you just can't stand the commute. And lastly, if you are working in a profession you absolutely can't stand but are doing it because your parents have pushed you into it as a career, get out! You will never be content. I've been fortunate enough to have parents support my career choices, and I've had a lot. But I've also had friends who are working a job they can't stand just to please their parents. If this is you, then you should be aware you are working purely to make your parents and not yourself happy. I would conjecture your parents would rather you be happy than making some extra money in a career they have chosen for you. If that's not the case, then ask yourself, "If my parents don't care about my happiness, then why do I care about their happiness?" It is your life and your choices, and it's on you to do what makes you happy. You are an adult now, free to make your own decisions. So take that, parents!

In the end, you need to control your career and not have your career control you by any external influence.

Knowing yourself and working for only you are the best ways to do that. And once you are in a company in a self-chosen career, keep your eyes and ears open to spot opportunities to make improvements. It could really take your workflow reputation up a notch.

Lastly, take time to engage your coworkers about their thoughts and feelings regarding the company. What you hear can be a great resource in your potential job-hopping decision making. It never hurts to have workplace friends; they may just give you that last push you need to pursue a career elsewhere.

What You Can Do Today

During downtime at work, create a list of all your company's direct competitors. List all the products they have, the services they offer, and if possible, the price points of them all. Then create a simple PowerPoint slide (preferably six slides or less) with easy to read charts and graphs that clearly shows where your company falls amongst the competition. Are you the cheapest? Are you the only one who can do X and Y? Are you missing out by not doing Q? Once you identify where your company is lacking and where your company is excelling in comparison to your competitors, take your data and share it with your boss, bosses, or bosse—a word I've just coined that is a "posse of bosses." Your findings probably may not be news to many, but seeing it presented in a different way may help trigger new ideas for improvement or be a subtle reminder to everyone else of where you stand amongst the competition. However, if your findings are news to many (or at least to one really important person), then you will shortly be in a bosse of your own and forever be on the star employee list.

This research should take you less than two hours to complete and can reap you many benefits. From your work on this simple assignment, you'll at least see the landscape of the company in a light that is probably consistent with the CEO. With a CEO mindset, you'll be able to filter your ideas for improvement and better understand why they will or won't work. In the end, you've just become a more valuable employee and most likely created a document that will be shared with all new hires for years to come. So make sure you put your name on the slide so you'll be forever remembered. If you so choose, lock it for editing.

For the unemployed, I recommend combing job listings not just for jobs, but for new skills, certificates, or education you may be lacking. Being unemployed offers you a ton of time, so take advantage of it. As unmotivated as you may be right now to do anything, if you make use of your time strategically, unemployment may be the best thing that ever happened to you career wise. Enrolling in free online classes via Coursera, Udacity, EdX, Khan Academy, Education Portal Academy, and other resources means you can take real classes taught by top colleges all for free. With Harvard or MIT certificates on your resume you'll stand out. With Duke and Stanford extracurricular learning, you'll be seen as an educated go-getter. These top-notch courses are free, online, and constantly covering new subjects, so check in often and enroll in as many as you can. Admittance is usually done on a first come, first serve basis. You can be a high school dropout and still take these classes. There is no interview process, lengthy application, or fees. Yes, a test is necessary to earn your certificate at the end of the class, but that's fine. Just study until you ace it. It's a great benefit to those with any free time, and it's a great resume-enhancer for frustrated job searchers. Plus, with the right attitude, learning new things can be fun! If a whole course seems too generic and you just want to learn a particular skill such as Photoshop, Excel, photography, or others, check out Lynda.com and CreativeLive.com. For a minimal monthly fee and around the clock classes, you can be a well-rounded applicant fairly quickly. In a matter of a few months, you could master a new employable skill set (instead of browsing Reddit and YouTube all day).

A great way to better prepare yourself for a successful job application is to find and bookmark a few similar job listings that are enticing to you for comparison. Then copy and paste the text of the descriptions and responsibilities of those jobs into a free, online word-cloud generator at Websites such as Wordle.net, Tagxedo.com, TagCrowd.com, or WordItOut.com. This will sort and display all the words by relative of importance. The more frequently the word is used, the larger the font it is given so it stands out more. Looking at the listings through this type of display makes it easy to see critical overlapping components for this particular job position, they are now written in the largest font. The smaller font items are less universally important in your field. Now you clearly know what you need to fit into the majority of these jobs. See, bigger is better. At least with fonts.

It's not enough that men have to get all the credit, they get a bigger paycheck too. A

Salary Science

study[1] from the nonprofit Catalyst, which focuses on advancing career opportunities for women, has found that women must approach their careers differently than men. Universally, women make 77 cents per every $1.00 that men make according to a study[2] by the National Partnership for Women & Families. The findings by Catalyst suggest the reason for this is that men are more likely to get paid for potential production, while women are more likely to get paid for past production. The study's findings show that men who job hop every few years can escalate their salaries quickly as they are continually evaluated according to the potential they may bring to a new company. Catalyst found men who switched from their first post-MBA job earned $13,743 more than those who stayed with their first company. Women on the other hand, usually end up making more money by staying with one job as long as possible and continually earning salary increases based on their tangible results. Catalyst showed women who changed jobs two or more times post-MBA ended up earning $53,472 less than women who rose through the ranks at their first job.

Sheryl Sandberg, who has been a C-level executive at both Google and Facebook, recently revealed in a New Yorker interview[3] that regardless of occupation women are possibly shooting themselves in the foot from the get-go. She said 57 percent of men negotiate their salaries upfront prior to starting a new position, while only 7 percent of women do so. Research[4] by Linda C. Babcock, a professor of economics at Carnegie Mellon University, makes a similar case that men are more likely to ask for more money. She ran experiments that assigned simple tasks to individuals with a stated payment range of eight to 13 dollars. When she paid the lowest amount in the range to every participant, men were eight times more likely than women to ask for more money. When she ran the experiment again and instead stated the pay was negotiable, men still asked for more money 30 percent more than women did. However, there seems to be a social reason for women instinctively accepting the pay that is offered. Babcock's additional studies showed that both men and women colleagues prefer working with women who don't negotiate. These women are considered more likable and easier to work with. So it appears women are aware they are judged differently and take on social risks when they ask for more pay. But as Laurel Thatcher Ulrich said, "Well-behaved women seldom make history." They probably make less money too.

University of Columbia research[5] has shown another factor in the payment discrepancy is that men tend to exaggerate their accomplishments more than women. (Men with egos? Perish the thought.) Men on average exaggerate their achievements by 30 percent, and women by 15 percent, which can make them seem like more attractive hires while job interviewing. It's not lying per se, it's that men usually exude more confidence and possibly believe they achieved more than they did while women report less embellished representations of their workplace achievements. Combining extra confidence (or lacking guilt for over-exaggerations), being paid on potential results rather than actual results, and then frequently switching jobs rather than becoming attached to one company can have tremendous effects on your salary as a man. So take this research and make it work best for you.

5

How Jill Can
Out-Earn Jack

While researching salaries in my free time after work, it was hard for me to find exact comparables to my title of Application Manager. It was obviously a custom title to cover various job responsibilities and not universally used by other companies. Joanna showed me a few job listings for software-related project manager roles that were offering $90,000 and beyond. Surprisingly, the listings requested the exact responsibilities and experience we were doing as part of our current jobs. I also found additional job listings with similar $90,000 pay days for the other roles our job entailed: quality assurance, client sales, and product manager. Here we were with basically four responsibilities at our current job, but if we only narrowed our focus into one of these roles and worked elsewhere, we could be making $20,000 more! It was a no-brainer that we both had to move on and explore other options at other jobs to increase our financial situations in the short-term and long-term. Our bitching was justified after all. But why would we make a higher salary if we were having fewer responsibilities and using a narrower skill set? It made no sense to get paid more for doing less. I had to dig deeper to find out why.

It reminded me of what I had learned about giving off the vibe as a "Jack-of-all-trades" on my resume: it is interpreted as "you must not do anything exceptionally well." Then it hit me that people who are Jacks-of-all-trades in any trade always get paid less than specialists of a trade. The Jacks, or do-everything types, are fairly good at a lot of different things, but not an expert at any one thing. They make a living off low margins (cheapest rate), but have high volume of work to keep them employed (can do everything under the sun). The experts, or what I'll call Jills-of-one-trade, work in low volume (there are only a few customers with this specific need), but earn a high margin on their work (will charge you a shitload of money to do it the best way possible).

The big bucks always go to a Jill, someone who is a rock star at one thing only. It's true in mechanics. If I take my car to my local service station, I know I'm going to get cheap and efficient service, no matter what car I bring them. They'll find a way to check the brakes, tires, and oil without compromising my car's overall safety. However, if I take it to the dealership, it'll cost way more, but I'm probably getting a better service. They'll know exactly what oil viscosity type to use, or get my tire pressured to the exact specifications of the owner's manual, or be on the lookout for any pre-determined faults my car may have. They are checking the exact same model of my car 50 times a day and thus can easily anticipate the issues it may have. Ultimately, my car will run better, as I may get an extra mile per gallon now, or extend the life of my car by a few thousand miles, or just provide me with additional overall safety for my car. It's on me to choose whether this extra expense is worth it. As a bargain hunter, I'd probably settle somewhere in the middle of the spectrum and go to an auto mechanic that caters to Japanese-manufactured hybrid cars only.

Doctors obviously work in niches to generate a higher income. A cardiologist gets paid more than a general practitioner. If you had a heart problem, would you pay extra to go to a heart expert? Hell yes, you would! Dr. Jill most likely has seen your problem before and knows instantly how to fix it. Dr. Jack, although his heart would be in the right place (pun groaners commence), will have you take several different types of medicines until he finds one that works.

So I started to see now that I had to narrow my focus in my day job too if I wanted a higher salary. Currently being a Jack at work did have its advantages, each day was something new. It also allowed me to test drive many different occupations at once. Being a Jack at work meant I didn't have to spend three months without a paycheck somewhere else to learn that QA and sales are not my cup of tea. My many responsibilities allowed me to learn I equally liked being a product manager and a project manager. So I focused on these two roles and went to devour job listings on these positions I wouldn't mind doing solely. I compared the skill sets, experience, roles and responsibilities of various product managers. Then I compared various project manager listings.

It seemed that the higher-paying product manager roles had various skill sets and qualifications. However, the project management roles all had similarly defined skill sets that mostly overlapped with one another like a Venn diagram. It was clear that if I focused on project management, I'd have a higher chance of being employed as I'd be qualified in more open positions. Venn for the win! I just had to get the basic criteria that each six-figure project management job listing mentioned: five to 10 years experience and an official project management certification.

Before I was able to review my findings with Joanna over lunch, she informed me she was going to pursue a career in project management also. She had her five years experience and decided to sign up to take the certification class to make her even more employable. The certification required making a $2,500 six-week class commitment, followed by a big test at the end. Her research had showed the same as mine: with her experience and this certification, there were a lot of openings that paid much more than either one of us were making now. Her missing piece to a big salary boost was this lone project management certificate, and she wanted to get it as fast as possible.

So I cobbled together my experience to see what I needed to do. I now had nine months experience at my current job working partly as a project manager—well short of the expected five years. However, I did do project management as my additional responsibilities at the electronic retailer I worked for, so that gave me about an extra six months of experience. Although I wasn't calling it project managing at the time, I did project manage the renovation of three houses my partners and I flipped during the real estate boom. I handled the budget, planning of resources, and scheduling. Same duties as I do now, just in the software business. In total, I had three years of project management experience, which was also the minimum necessary to take the project management certification classes. So I signed up for them right along with Joanna.

Joanna now had her clear path to riches. She slyly inquired to Don to see if our company would cover the cost of her training, but it got rejected. Even so, she moved ahead with taking the class on her own dime. Sure, it cost a lot of money, but she'd make that back quickly with a bigger paycheck at her next gig. My path to riches was going to be a little longer, as I would have to get my certification and then hang around my current job for two more years to earn the extra experience. I was absolutely not willing to remain at my current gig for that long. I knew once Joanna left, all her workload would fall on me. Knowing how the company operated, this extra workload would not come with extra compensation either. I needed to shorten my path to riches and get out as fast as possible too. Jumpin' Jehoshaphat, I'm jumpin' jobs again!

I decided if I couldn't expedite my experience at the moment, that I could at least double-up on my education. I found another certification that worked well with the general project management certification class Joanna and I were both taking. This second class cost $1,500, was three days long, and only focused on how to be a project manager in software using a new technique called Agile. If I could earn both of these certifications, I would create an even more specific niche for my occupation. I wouldn't be just a project manager and I wouldn't be just a software project manager, I would be an Agile software project manager. I wasn't exactly sure how difficult it would be to get the Agile certification, but online job listings confirmed having this even narrower focus would earn an even higher pay day than a more generic project manager would make. I decided right then to make this my career path. I figured my extra education would make up for my lacking experience. I secretly hoped this would be my express jet to making $100,000. Then it hit me: I had just accidently stumbled into something that I could see myself doing for a career. And one that I actually enjoyed! I couldn't believe it. This was a win-win all around.

Eight weeks later, after some long nights of studying, Joanna and I aced our project management tests. We both knew that her days at our company were now limited. There was so much more out there she could do now, and it paid so much better. While she started her job search, I took three days off from work to attend my second certification classes. I was spending my hard-earned vacation days and my depleted savings to take this class, but I knew my reward for doing so would come soon enough. The salary jump I would get more than covered the costs of both of my certification classes combined. My research showed going this route would be more beneficial than getting a $50,000-a-year MBA or a Masters diploma from a university, which was another way I could have doubled up on my education. The diploma route would take two years and require me to be paying back loans for decades. Certified classes took weeks to earn, were priced considerably less, and also could land me top-paying jobs instantly. Spending your money on education can be one of the safest investments, but you still need to thoroughly research where you get educated. My situation, or career prospects, would not improve any more if I had chosen to take the "traditional" route to earning higher education.

When I returned the following week, Joanna had already put in her two weeks' notice! She had started interviewing while taking her certification classes, putting on her resume she would be certified by a certain date. Now that she passed, she had a new gig waiting for her as a software project manager that was paying her $90,000. Her $2,500 investment in her education resulted in a $28,000 pay raise. (That's an ROI of 1,020 percent. Not bad, as ROIs go.) I was ecstatic for her. It also confirmed we were doing the right thing by investing in ourselves and looking elsewhere for new opportunities. I was so proud of her; she worked hard and improved her situation. And her quick movements had motivated me to do the same. I just wished I had started my job hunt pre-certification as well.

Subversive Job Tip

If you don't have time to send out resume after resume and tailor a cover letter to match, then have someone do it for you by outsourcing your job hunt. Using freelance Websites such as Odesk.com and Elance.com, you can hire someone overseas to do this for you for less than 2 dollars an hour. Make sure they do the work as if they are you and under your name. You can give them free reign to do as they please or implement a cover letter approval system before each submission. Offer a $50 bonus for any interview they arrange. It's now in their best interest to do the best job possible. Bonus Points: Outsource your networking too by getting someone to arrange strategic introductions for you, manage your Twitter account with engaging industry specific tweets, or even create a daily blog post on your behalf.

After Joanna's last day, Don pulled me into this office. He wanted to know why Joanna had left, he thought everything was going great with her. Now I was feeling super confident in my position with the company, more secure than I ever felt as an employee before. For one, Don was desperate and was looking for me to shoulder Joanna's workload until her replacement could be hired and trained. Secondly, I had the self-assurance of someone who now had two new certifications that made me highly employable and worthy of a higher salary. Finally, I had validation that I was on path to earn $90,000 once I earned a little more experience. With my newfound confidence, I figured if the opportunity presented itself, maybe I could parlay Joanna's leaving into financially benefitting me.

It didn't take long for me to get there. As I sat down, I explained, "Well, Joanna got an offer to just do project management that paid almost $30,000 more. It's because we both got our certification last week and that is highly valued in the marketplace right now." A bit of a shock came across his face, and his concern now was if I was going to leave too. I followed with, "Well, of course, it makes sense for me to at least test the waters too—that's a lot of money. I just spent my vacation days to get an additional certificate, because I think that it will really help the company. I saw other people's companies were paying for it, and I knew we weren't in a position to do that, but I really wanted to perform better in my current role here, so I invested in it myself." Now, without me saying so he knew instantly my explanation was complete bullshit and that I was obviously doing all that I could to get out as soon as possible. However, he took the threat seriously, and I was blown away with what happened next. Don instantly gave me a $15,000 raise to bring my salary up to $85,000 and also offered to reimburse me for my latest $1,500 course. On top of that, he also credited back my three vacation days. Jesus H. Income! My attempt to parlay Joanna's exit into ben-efitting me couldn't have worked out any better. I was now just $15,000 away from six figures. Checking the calendar, I saw I had two and half months to finagle my way somehow to $100,000! It now seemed legitimately achievable. My investment in education did pay off and right away, too. I was so overjoyed I even smiled all through a week's worth of lunches.

Subversive Job Search 101

At a certain point in your career you will need to have a specialty in order to earn a bigger pay day. Would you want to hire a person that was exclusively a project manager for three years or some-one who did it part time with a bunch of other respon-sibilities for six years? I would say the safer, less risky, and more skilled employee would be the project man-ager with experience in a very specific focus. He shows he's dedicated to the craft, has relevant knowledge, and wants to do more of it. Thinking of what I did at work through a different lens helped me narrow and choose a career focus. If I hadn't done that, I would still be a Jack-of-all-trades making much less money. Narrowing my professional choices to become a Jill would be the best career move I could make.

Greg McKeown wrote an excellent blog entry[1] for the Harvard Business Review called "The Disciplined Pursuit of Less." He speculates on why successful people do not always succeed everywhere they go. And he put it in four phases:

1. When we *really* have clarity of purpose, it leads to success.

2. When we have success, it leads to more options and opportunities.

3. When we have increased options and opportunities, it leads to diffused efforts.

4. Diffused efforts undermine the very clarity that led to our success in the first place.

An example of what McKeown is saying is that Michael Jordan had an unbelievably ambitious drive to be the best basketball player in the world. That clarity of a specific focus drove every decision he made until he achieved greatness. Because of this, he is unquestionably the best basketball player to have ever lived. Once he achieved expert status, he now had options. He could go try to be the best poker player, the best baseball player, the best golfer, and more. His success in basketball now allowed him to pursue greatness in other fields if he so chose. And he did pursue, and like anyone, he wanted to try them all out. Jordan diffused his focus, and thus, he didn't automatically become hugely successful in everything he touched. This diffusion ultimately led to mixed results. His baseball career was below-average. His gambling losses were unimaginable. However his golf game is pretty impressive. MJ's focus was now all over the map, and so were his successes. It's his prerogative obviously, but he never would have been considered the best basketball player ever if he tried to do all these things before he had earned that title.

You think Michael Phelps would have won 22 Olympic swimming medals if he was also trying to learn how to be a five-star chef at the same time? Do you think Steve Jobs would have made Apple the biggest tech company if he was also pursuing an acting career? Take a look at your career choices and decisions. Are you all over the map too? Do you have a singular focus? If you do everything you can to excel at one small thing and own it as your specialty, you'll eventually be rewarded for it. Maybe that reward will be getting paid top dollar doing what you do best. Maybe that reward will put you in position to pursue opportunities to excel in other fields too. Figure out what reward you want and go for it.

You are the only one directly in control of your career. It's not your boss. It's not your loved ones. It's not the company you work for. It's you. If you want a more balanced work life and like to bounce all over the place, that's perfectly okay. Understand that it may compromise your pay, but if that doesn't bother you then keep doing it. It may even help you find where you fit best. If you see in comparable job listings you are lacking some highly sought-after skills, it's on you to learn these and get up to date. Always ask your employer first to see if they will cover the costs of acquiring new skills. This shows you want to be a better employee and that you care about not only your job, but your career. Worst case scenario, they say no and then you find a way to do it on your own dime. Investing in you first is always the right answer. You should never regret that decision.

Once again, having confidence and noticing when others are vulnerable are your biggest allies when asking for a raise. I knew I was in the power position once Joanna left as I had to start doing two people's work until they found a replacement. Thankfully, my boss wanted to make sure I was happy, and he did everything he could to keep me around. I give him a lot of credit for that. But if I didn't go into a meeting prepared to slightly hint at a potential departure of my own, that conversation and resulting raise may not have ever happened. By taking charge of my own career, I was justly rewarded.

Take a page out of Joanna's book and put on your resume your expected completion date of all your certifications or course work. This way you can get a jumpstart on your job search while you are getting certified, rather than waiting until you've completed everything you are working on. Even if it's nine to 12 months in advance, it's perfectly acceptable to mention it on your resume. You can discuss how you'll balance both your job and the remaining course work you have once you get an interview (an interview that you wouldn't have had if you had waited to start your job hunt until you were done with your work).

Look at the job listings of the six-figure job you want. If the only thing keeping you from

What You Can Do Today

it is less-than-stellar education or certification, then I recommend cheap education over expensive education (unless your work is paying for it). I'm not a fan of MBA or other advanced college degree programs. I think spending $50,000 or more on an advanced diploma is best served in other ways. Take that $50,000 and start your own business for two years. I promise you'll earn much more real-world experience than what can be taught from a textbook. Alternative and cheaper educations I do support. Along with the free university courses mentioned previously in this chapter, you can also acquire career specific knowledge via certifications, seminars, conferences, and Webcasts. You not only get laser-focused niche knowledge, but you also create a bigger swath of networking opportunities by attending a lot of different events regularly, each one possibly targeting slightly different audiences. I firmly believe "it's who you know" in the long scheme of things, so try to meet as many people as possible, even if it's just an online introduction.

If you have no clue how to start a business, it's the same as my working-for-free advice as before. A great way to start would be to find a starving, unknown, or amateur artist, performer, or creative person you really like and volunteer to help her out. Do you want be in artist management? Offer to book a three-city tour for her. Do you want to be in public relations? Offer to send out some press releases on her behalf. Do you want to be a graphic artist? Offer to do her Website, stickers, album covers, and more. Do you want to be a set designer? Then build her a great stage. Trust me, working for free is the best plan of action when you have no other way to get your foot in the door. And continue doing free awesome work for her as long as you can. Once you succeed and she's happy with the results, she'll recommend you to other artists. You can charge the next artist a few bucks and then you again do knock-out work. And then the next one a few bucks more and make it so impressive she'll start talking to others about you. And before you know it, you are the local go-to person for whatever skill you are honing and are now running a legit business based on a whirl-wind of word-of-mouth referrals. Any business owner in the world would not only be successful with that sort of free publicity, but could quickly become a highly sought after expert ready to earn a big income. And if one of those artists you helped takes off and makes it big (probably the same chance as a startup of making it big), you are sitting pretty with a whole new network of celebrity referrals.

You don't need to quit your day job to start a side business or dip your toe in the water of a new occupation. I've started and created at least 10 businesses while keeping my day job over the years. None of them ever required my full attention at the beginning. Once they did, then I would have considered quitting my day job and doing it full-time, but that has never happened. Many times I learned there wasn't really a marketplace for what I was working on, the business was too work intensive and not easily scalable, or that my heart really wasn't in to it. These learning lessons allowed me to continue trying new things without completely abandoning my steady income at the day gig. It's okay to dip your toe in the water of being an entrepreneur, but don't go full throttle unless your new business is so successful that it starts to demand it.

Salary Science

A 2011 Accenture survey[2] found that only 21 percent of U.S. employees had received any employer-provided formal training in the past five years. So the expectation for a majority of employees should be that your job will not pay for your training and education; these are skills that you are responsible for. The office as a classroom mentality has officially changed.

If you already have or just began acquiring an MBA, don't fret. This is obviously a valuable and impressive degree to have earned. I just don't advocate digging yourself into an asinine amount of debt to achieve it without having a solid career plan already in place. If an advanced business degree is in your future, you should do everything you possibly can to do scholarly research work. University of Tennessee–Knoxville professor Russell Crook's research[3] found that those that did academic research in business school earned a higher salary over non-researching graduate students. His conclusions were that this type of work gave students additional knowledge, honed their skills and abilities, and prepared them for the real world. With this increased arsenal of skills, research students earned as much as $24,000 a year more than other students without this experience. The subject matter that they researched didn't really matter; it's just having done it that propelled these students' careers and earned them a 21 percent increase in salary just three years later. This type of work in graduate school is a great way to start earning a decent return on a potentially very expensive investment.

Now many students earn a degree in something completely different than their eventual career. Let's take a look at college education, as this book is also about "overcoming your useless degree." Did you know that above-average IQ individuals are only 1.2 times as likely as below-average IQ individuals to achieve a high net worth?[4] It's important to comprehend that a whole lotta dumb people can get rich too. That's a mere 20 percent if my below-average arithmetic is correct. It's not all about your brains. Imagine having dinner with Snookie, Paris Hilton, and R. Kelly. Are you the richest one at the table? Not even close. Are you the smartest one? Hell yes. (You're reading a book aren't you?) So know there are ways to the top besides being studious.

However, there are some demographics that are highly encouraged to get a college degree based on the results of a recent UCLA-led study.[5] The study found that the highest economic return for attending college is earned by students who were identified as least likely to go. Students of color from low-income backgrounds benefited the most by earning a college degree. If you find yourself in this situation, it's a boon for you to attend a university as males are likely to earn 30 percent more and females 35 percent more than your peers who didn't go to college. A college education is worth two to three times more for disadvantaged students than it is for privileged college-goers. The reasoning is that high school graduates from disadvantaged backgrounds face a much tougher labor market than graduates from a privileged background. A privileged student who has parents that went to college and has friends that went to college already has a social network that can be leveraged for employment. They are surrounded by educated and connected people. These social connections, or lack thereof, should be the main criteria in determining if college is the right option for you.

6

Brand New Branding

Your brand is what people say about
you when you're not in the room.

—Jeff Bezos[1]

As great as I felt about the way my company had
handled my feedback, the new raise didn't stop me from
trying out the job market. I was going to climb my way
to $100,000 one way or another, and I wanted to do it
quickly. Joanna got a $30,000 raise in less than a week
after earning her certification. I had to know what was
out there for me; maybe I could do the same. Exploding
with confidence, I decided to rebrand myself as the expert I needed to be to get the big bucks. I didn't have
five to 10 years project management experience, but I
did have 10 years of software experience. I also had
international experience, having worked with clients,
sub-contractors, and internal teams that were distrib-
uted across the globe in various jobs throughout my

life. Now I was not only certified as a project manager, but also in the smaller component of it called Agile. If I wanted to get paid like an expert, I had to be seen as an expert. The best way to do that was to own this very narrow career niche that I had accidently stumbled into.

In previous jobs, I've had to interview and hire people to work on my team. Having experienced being the hiring manager has actually helped me quite a bit when I found myself sitting on the other side of the table. I've met with candidates who have had excellent resumes and had aced their initial phone interviews, but I ended up not pursuing them. I'm sure they've wondered what the hell went wrong when they didn't get the job in the end. The most common reason is because their online presence gave me a muddled brand of themselves. I'm not talking about finding a random drunk photo posted by a friend that was obviously inappropriate, but something an applicant has done, created, and promoted himself outside of the interview. For example, hard-working Joe Schmo, generically named job-seeker, applied to a position within my company. His resume looks impressive so I set up a phone call. The phone conversation goes even better, so I go with the next step of trying to learn more about him before I call him in for an in-person interview. I somehow end up at his Website at JoeSchmo.com because I either Googled his name, he provided his Website on his resume, or maybe it was just revealed in his e-mail address (joe@joeschmo.com). Now when I go to the Website the title in big letters says "Joe Schmo—Actor, Programmer, and

Handyman." I now have a better picture of Joe and I see his true career bio. Or more accurately, his personal brand. Now, what job at my company do you think he applied for?

It doesn't matter; I would never hire Joe Schmo for anything important. If I was a director of a Broadway play, I would not cast someone who is not purely dedicated to the craft of acting. I'd want passionate actors that would reflect my passion of directing. If I was running a software company, I'd want someone who lives and breathes programming. I wouldn't want someone who *can* program; I'd want someone who *wants* to do nothing but code all day long. A handyman is a jack-of-all trades that will rarely earn prestigious assignments. I may hire him to do a small task here and there, but nothing that I would consider super important or super expensive. I would go to him only if I needed the cheapest quote possible. Joe is subconsciously telling me he has the skills to do pretty much any construction job, but they aren't good enough to make it a full-time career or to be an expert in anything.

However, if I'm directing a local volunteer stage production that will probably be seen by about 10 people, Joe is my man. I know I could probably get Joe Schmo to act in it, build the stage, and build the Website. I just filled three jobs for the price of none (if Joe volunteers as well). Joe only gets the gig(s) because he can do everything decent enough to get by. You get what you pay for. My expectations are low, and so I pay him a low rate. If he accepts this gig, he'll be running in circles, his focus is all over the place, and his work will most likely suffer from it. This is different than working for free on just one specific task. Then I would expect spectacular work if he wants to earn a referral.

Allow me to switch gears for a second and approach this with a hypothetical question. Would you drink Coke Juice? Strange question, but really if I gave you a red and white can that says orange juice under the Coca-Cola logo, would you want to drink it for breakfast with your eggs and bacon every morning? After making a WTF face, you'd probably ask me if it's carbonated. Then ask me if it is brown or orange. Is it a mix of the two? Then you'd ask does it have corn syrup in it? Is there pulp? Is it disgusting? And on and on and on, and then after you get all your questions out you'll be mad because your eggs and bacon have gotten cold. I'd finally put the can of Coke Juice back in the fridge and bring you a bottle of Minute Maid orange juice. And you'd say, "Why didn't you do that the first time?" and call me some choice words that probably shouldn't be spoken so early in the morning. I'd say I did bring that out to you the first time and you asked a million questions! And then you'd make that WTF face again. I know this because this was what transpired when I tried this on my wife.

You see, Minute Maid is the brand of The Coca-Cola Company's juice line. Coca-Cola is the brand name for their best selling soft drink. The Coca-Cola Company has many brand names for their many different products, and they are smart enough to differentiate them all. You may pass on a bottle of Coca-Cola water, but you'll probably drink a bottle of Dasani with no problem. You may pass on a Coca-Cola sports drink, but not on Powerade. And the same goes for Coca-Cola juice and Minute Maid. The Coca-Cola Company has clear concise brands, all with different names across the different markets it serves. You also need to do the same.

Your name is your brand as well as your online persona. And your brand creates the foundation for your career. So what should Joe Schmo do? Obviously everyone has interests outside of their job, just don't advertise them. Of course we will all be in different levels of our career and can't always follow our passion full-time, but don't tell me about it. One solution for Joe would be to separate all his online mediums into different occupations. He could use his Website for just his construction persona, and I'd recommend he focuses further on a specialty that he enjoys. Maybe it is high-end banisters, custom garages, or even roofing. Find a niche and own it. Joe then could use LinkedIn for just his programming circle of contacts and to promote his programming resume. Joe could use Facebook just for his non-work friends and then use Twitter just for acting. If he does this and I Google "Joe Schmo actor" I will only find his Twitter account. If I only Google "Joe Schmo" and it returns all his occupations, then I'm likely to dismiss the other accounts as belonging to different Joe Schmos.

Also, time and resource permitting, a more long-term strategic route would be for Joe to create multiple identities. Maybe he goes by the name Joe Schmo when he is doing construction, Joe Michael Schmo when he is an actor, Joe M. Schmo when he is the programmer, and J. Michael Schmo when he is a customer service rep, the job he applied for. That's a lot to keep up with, but also keeps everything separate and opens up the door for the furthest career advancement in each field. Of course he would need a business card, resume, and Website to match each of his personal brands! And they should all be designed differently, each one with unique colors and styles. Having them all look the same would undo all the work he's done.

I have the same problem and I identified this problem too late. I'm Alan Corey the financial and career author. I'm Alan Corey the real estate investor. I'm Alan Corey the project manager. I've also created a TV pilot about sports, I've created a Web start-up about NYC schools, I'm an Improv Everywhere prankster. I've been Alan Corey the comedian, the bar owner, the reality TV show regular, and more. My identity should be one large bottle of Coke Juice that no one will drink, and at times it probably is.

I now work hard to keep all my careers separate when necessary and merge them as little as possible. Having multiple and separate identities would have been so much easier for me from the beginning, but it's too late for me to switch now. You'd probably still read this book if it was written by A.M. Corey or Corey Alan, right? But you wouldn't easily make the connection that I'm the same author you may have already read because I published the first book under the name of Alan Corey. I'm committed now. You bet I'm holding myself back by not focusing on just one single profession in my branding, and I'm most likely financially paying the price.

Here is how I'm handling it. To be as successful as possible in new fields, I work on only one big project at a time. If I'm trying to get a book deal, I reflect this across all my online profiles. My Tweets become book-based, my bio only mentions my writing credentials, and more. When I'm working on finding a project management job, I replace everything with technology and project management banter and remove everything that is not. Being a bit of an Internet chameleon helps me further one brand at a time in whatever I'm doing at that moment. I make sure online I'm one thing at a time and not ten things at a time. It's not perfect and it's a helluva lot more work than if I differentiated from the beginning, but it's an improvement over what Joe Schmo is doing.

My personal brand now is really an average guy who lives multiple lives, sometimes at once, and tells his readers about how they can do it for maximum financial benefit. A running joke among my friends is that I have a brand new career every six months and they can't keep up with me. That's what my first book was about, and it turns out that is what this book is about. So that blending, reinventing, and then storytelling are what people have begun to expect from me. I know this because the number-one search term that gets people to my site is "What is Alan Corey doing now?" That tells me they expect to find me doing something different, unique, or impressive. And they want to read about it. (That or I have one determined stalker who needs a daily update on my actions.) But I couldn't do all these things if I didn't first have the singular focus of being a millionaire before 30. Having that clarity of vision led me to success, and that success has now opened up doors elsewhere and provided me some career flexibility.

Where I draw the line is in my corporate career. When I'm at work as a project manager, it's a different story. I don't say a word about anything outside project management. I don't put my Website on my resume. When I go to dinners invited by work friends, I stay in project management mode. I've created separate circles of contacts and friends, and I rarely merge them unless necessary. Because of it, people in my office don't Google me. Why would they want to learn more about this boring work-first project management freak? Why would they ever think I have a Web presence outside of LinkedIn? To them, I'm just a worker bee. I've worked at four jobs and interviewed at about 10 others in the past 18 months, and no one has ever asked me about anything outside my streamlined and laser-focused resume. They either didn't Google me beforehand, Googled me and didn't care, or Googled me and thought it was a different Alan Corey. If I have two different personas going at once, then I use different photos and design schemes to differentiate them. If they found me online representing one of my other career brands, the message they got was probably so foreign compared to the resume they were holding in their hand they knew it had to have been someone else. I've worked hard at being one brand at a time, and it has been hugely successful for me. If my different online identities were all grouped together, then I'm positive it would have held me back in all my careers and I'd probably still be on unemployment.

Subversive Job Tip

Create a free Google Alert of your name. You'll get pinged with an e-mail every time your name shows up on the Web. This is an excellent way to track your online identity, manage your brand, and see first what others may find out about you. Bonus Points: Identify a hard-to-reach person you would like to work for and assume they have a Google alert of their name too. Create a webpage or blog post that is an open letter to them that addresses why you'd be the perfect hire. You should mention you know of subversive ways to get others to notice you. Done poorly, you are dismissed as creepy. Done well, you are called in for an interview.

Eventually people do find out about my other interests. It usually takes about nine months into a day job for this to happen. Maybe they read something about me somewhere, saw me being interviewed on television, or I said something with my guard down to a co-worker. I answer honestly that yes, I do that on the side as a hobby. No one cares at that point because I've already been hired, and obviously it doesn't distract from my work as it took them nine months to find out. But the company would have never hired me if that was the message I was sending out come interview time. Who wants a can of Coke Juice walking around the office? It took me 10 years to learn to live my brand only within that brand's environment. Maybe if I knew that before, I would have been at six-figures long ago.

Now that I was in a project management mode trying to find a new job, I worked on creating a one to two sentence bio of myself, sometimes called a USP or Unique Selling Proposition. This USP would be used on my LinkedIn profile to identify me as an expert project manager. From there, I built a resume and a matching online persona to avoid any cross-contamination of my personal brands. To ensure success, I was effectively only Alan Corey the project manager now.

I played around with a lot of different project management work bios and narrowed it down to two:

A. Certified project manager with a strong software background and international experience.

B. PMP and Agile/Scrum certified project manager and 10-year international software professional.

I was both A and B, but the phrasing of the second one made me the low-risk industry veteran worthy of the big bucks. PMP was the acronym for the Project Management Profession certification I earned and what I anticipated was most likely the main search term a recruiter would use to find me. (Though 50 Cent is a P.I.M.P., I'm just a PMP. Wayyy less cool.) Agile and Scrum were potential key terms for other recruiters to find me as well, and it reflected my second certification. I followed this with my 10 years in software line as a bit of a hint that I've been around a long time even if it was not all spent in project management. I was now confident that this bio screamed "solid hire" that enjoys this line of work.

I further rebranded my resume by replacing my customer service experience at the electronics company with my project management experience. I listed all the items that I project managed there and made those items the highlight. The customer service success was now a minor point of my time spent there. So minor, I even removed Customer Service Manager from my title and replaced it with Project Manager. To be clear, I wasn't lying on my resume, I was repackaging it. To be on the safe side, I ended up putting as a minor point on my resume that I was originally hired as Customer Service Manager, even though I didn't think it was necessary for me to do that. In potential interviews, I would be upfront and honest if asked about my time there. I would inform them I was hired to be Customer Service Manager; I had such early success at it, that I was given additional project management tasks that became the majority of my daily workload. Because of this, my title was an inaccurate reflection of my work duties and responsibilities, and I felt like it gave the wrong impression on my resume.

As an added layer of protection, I e-mailed the CEO at my old company asking if I could use him as a reference. Yes, the one that hastily fired me one day before I was due a huge bonus. I let him know what my new career direction was, and I reminded him of all the project management tasks I did while working there. I also informed him that I'm not even putting customer service on my resume due to how we had ended things. From his viewpoint, he had no trouble agreeing that customer service was not for me (even though his ratings were now back to 94 percent). He was relieved I had found a new line of work and he gave me his blessing in providing a referral for my project management work. He had no qualms with how I handled those tasks.

Seeing this slight change on my resume felt really good. I now truly appeared as the project manager expert I needed to be. I had my new narrow niche defined, my branding to match, and it was time to officially hit the job market. With this alignment, I imagined I'd instantly appear as a six-figure employee to any hiring manager. It was perfect timing too; I was only two months away from my approaching deadline of reaching just that milestone.

The next step to further identify myself within this niche was to find a job listings Website to match my skill set. Monster.com and HotJobs.com were for everyone. It was too crowded for an expert with a specialty like me now. So I went with the job-listing site Dice.com, as it had a niche of its own: tech jobs only. I also hit TheLadders.com, a site dedicated to only job listings that paid $100,000 or more. If all went as planned, this was going to be my moment to shine.

Dice.com proved to be the better fit for me. After three days, I even had to take my public resume off the site. I had more than 20 recruiters calling me with potential job interviews! I imagine this is what a hot girl feels like in a frat bar. It was annoying to get so much positive attention. (Yes, I always find a way to complain about how awesome things are going for me.) I was spending so much of my day fielding calls and e-mails about jobs all over the tri-state area that I couldn't get my work done at my current job. So to screen all the recruiters, I made a wish list and started making requirements. I didn't want to waste the recruiter's time, and I didn't want to waste my time. On first contact I made it clear I currently had a job I enjoyed (makes me sound less desperate) and that I would be looking to leave it for a position that paid more than $100,000. I also stated I'm only looking for positions located in

New York City within my niche of Agile project management. Additionally, I put in a request that I'd love to deal with international teams, if possible, however it was not a deal breaker. This was very specific, and it greatly reduced the number of calls I was getting; I was now in the driver's seat. The recruiters would only now reach out to me if they had an exact match, and I knew that match existed as I'd seen a few online listings about it during my salary research. It was just a matter of time before my perfect job surfaced; I just had to stick to my new repackaged persona. I sent some Hail Marys to Buck Greenback, as by now I only had six weeks left to meet my six-figure goal. Hail Buck, full of grace!

Subversive Job Search 101

Even if you are comfortable at your current job, it is still a good idea to update your resume and potentially go on interviews. At the very least, occasionally upload it to job-listing sites that have a public resume database. This simple act costs nothing, and you'll gain huge insights on how employable you are at any moment in time. This potential wake-up call can tell you what skills you are lacking, or any additional training you may need. It may alert you to the fact you are underpaid, have a really bad resume, or maybe that you are in high demand. You should always be prepared to start a job search as your company may go under, or you have to move to a new state, or some other factor that you cannot anticipate. Being ready with a back-up plan is a sure fire way to never have to miss a paycheck. And if you do this and you learn you are happy and paid well at your current job, then no harm done! Confirming you are getting paid more than you are worth should at least make your worst days in the office just a little more bearable.

Find and locate career-specific job-listing Websites and create a public resume. Being a part of your career's community will help with your job hunting, even if it's just using their job-listing services. You do not necessarily need to avoid the larger and more generic job-listing sites, but avoiding the niche ones can be costly. It doesn't hurt to have many people know about you, so try to be easily found. If you are hesitant to do this and are worried about being "caught" looking for a job by your current boss, you can make your resume anonymous or even black out your current job. Hiring managers and recruiters will understand. However, if you are a great worker and your employer knows you are looking elsewhere, they will most likely do whatever they can to keep you happy. My experience shows with the right moves you could parlay this into a $15,000 raise and more.

Creating your career bio in the form of a one- to two-sentence recap forces you to identify and highlight your strengths. The trick is make it specific and tailored to one career. Doing this gives you a starting point for your personal brand. Without a bio, it's hard to know where you've been. If you show where you've been within your career, a hiring manager can conclude where you want to go. If someone searches for you online, you want to control the message that they get and doing the above is the best way to do that.

If you are rebranding, don't forget you have to be able to back up the new brand. If you are using a former colleague or boss as a recommendation, you must alert them of your new career direction. Make sure he or she is comfortable making the recommendations that match it. If you don't, they may muddle your brand just as bad as Joe Schmo did with his Website. If there is no truth to your brand, then your brand is a house of cards that will eventually derail your career. Being trustworthy is a key element to any brand, personal or not. It can be the difference of having a high-paying job or no job at all. Unsubstantiated claims on a resume are a career dead end. If you are uncomfortable about repackaging your resume by putting in a more realistic title of the work you actually performed, you are putting yourself at a disadvantage. Like it or not, it is what your competition is doing, and it has become a necessity. If you can't back it up in an interview (or in a work environment), then you know you've gone too far.

What You Can Do Today

Google yourself right now. What do you find? What do you think about the person you are reading about? Try to think objectively. Are you Coke Juice? Are you nowhere to be found? Both of these are absolute no-nos. You have to have an online presence and you have to be an expert in a single field. Once you brand yourself an expert, you are on your way to being a big fish in a small pond. It's obvious, but worth stating: the best paying jobs usually go to the person best fit for that job. You can do that by concentrating on niche job-listing Websites within your industry. If you are the best graphic artist on a graphic artist only resume Website, then you are going to be paid top dollar. You may get lost in a shuffle or under-appreciated in the everything-under-the-sun Websites with millions of resumes.

Upload your resume to a few different Websites and see where you are getting the most traction. Usually a recruiter checks weekly to see the newest resumes online, so you'll get most of your calls that first week. Many might assume if your resume was uploaded six months ago that you've found a job and moved on, or rightly assume your resume is out of date. If you are currently employed and you don't get any calls from a recruiter within 14 days, your resume or your branding is probably wrong. This is another good way to A/B test your resume without having to send out hundreds of e-mails.

A good exercise to go with your personal branding is to have a mental career wish list that includes location, job responsibilities, company culture, and expected pay. Always work toward this wish list one way or another. Maybe you are at the beginning of your career and can't be too picky, but as you gain experience, you should get more specific and detailed on your career must-haves and goals. This wish list is expected to evolve over time, so constantly revaluate it. The more expertise you gain, the more you need to control your career. Otherwise your career will be controlled by your boss or a recruiter looking for a referral fee.

If you can't find a career-specific site for what you do or your resume is too limited, talk to someone who has the job you want. Ask them to be your mentor. Find out from them what skills you should learn, and ask them to share how they got started doing what they are doing. They will be most likely be flattered by the attention. Just reaching out can prove to be a career-changing move. Check in every six to 12 months for their advice and recommendations. Knowing as many people as possible in your career field can pay huge dividends. You never know when a job will open up with your name on it. If the right people know you are eager and interested in a certain job, they'll be more than happy to recommend you. This behind-the-scenes networking happens more than you think, so do what you can to be a part of it. (Actually an ExecuNet.com poll[2] found seven out of 10 six-figure jobs were found through networking.)

As your first and last name is most likely not a corporate brand, it's important to under-

stand what makes a good personal brand. You don't have a logo, you have your reputation. You probably don't have marketing materials; instead, you have your online profile. If you don't have much of any of the above, then your personal brand is your personality. So let's look at some slight personality tweaks that can help you make more money.

Being popular pays the big bucks. If you were considered popular in high school, you are likely to earn 10 percent more than those who were not considered popular.[3] A working paper[4] from the Institute for Social and Economic Research found that every friend one had in high school correlated to a 2 percent salary increase as an adult. To be clear, that is people who considered you their friend, not how many friends you had. So it pays to be nice and friendly.

For flirty women, your sexual overtones are costing you big bucks. A Tulane University study[5] found that overly flirtatious women with MBAs who even occasionally dress provocatively by highlighting their cleavage or wearing short skirts are not respected in the office place. Inappropriate actions like commenting on another's appearance, hinting at a potential attraction, or even a shoulder massage results in these women being considered a flirt. The study found that an MBA-holding flirt's salary range usually tops out at $75,000. Women with MBAs who do not partake in any of these overt acts are more likely to earn salaries in the $75,000–$100,000 range.

A University of North Carolina–Chapel Hill paper[6] has demonstrated that lack of sleep can cause deviant behavior at work. Working long hours on little to no sleep will reduce your self-control and increase hostility, which can even be noticed by colleagues through e-mail. And if your lack of self-control starts with having a spirited tongue, it can be costly. A Career Builder survey[7] of bosses showed that the majority of bosses (57 percent) said they are less likely to promote someone who curses. A larger percentage (64 percent) admits to thinking less of an employee who habitually swears. The reasons cited are that swearing brings into question an employee's professionalism (81 percent), self-control (71 percent), and maturity (68 percent). Some of these mothertruckin' bosses say it makes you appear more dumber (54 percent). Dang. The survey also identified what cities had the highest inner-office swearing occurring. So if you live in Washington, DC (62 percent), Denver (60 percent), or Chicago (58 percent), then you have the best chance of leaving a big impression just by keeping a mouth that your mother would kiss.

But what about bosses who swear? A University of Iowa study[8] found that abusive bosses who swear and verbally attack employees don't suffer for their bad behavior as long as they are producing positive results. The abuse is seen as acceptable by third-party colleagues as it is considered effective and productive. So if you have a verbally abusive boss, you could just stop doing good work. Then his tactics will be called into question and he'll be fired—but probably after you get fired first.

7

Contractor Cash Cow

I'm tired of hearing about money, money, money, money, money. I just want to play the game, drink Pepsi, and wear Reebok.

—Shaquille O'Neal

One night I was sharing my career updates with my friend Rich over dinner. As I was telling him how my recent certifications were helping me define my career and they were a major factor to my recent raise, he stopped me. He had a friend who was a recruiter looking to hire someone immediately for a software project manager role with these same qualifications. However, it required someone with experience in the media industry.

If you asked me point blank, I would say no, I've never had media experience as I've never worked for a media company. However, during the years I've been assigned clients that worked at the *New York Times*, at a South American TV station, and one at a local news

Website. Those were definitely media companies, and I asked Rich if that counted as actual media industry experience. He wasn't sure, but he told me to put it in a resume and he'll forward it on to his friend. He only knew a few details, but thought it was worth it for me to find out more.

So I went to work creating what felt like the 400th version of my resume. This time I put in my possible media experience, branded myself the best that I could as a media-focused software project manager, and updated my online personas to match. I thought I was really pushing the envelope here, trying to stretch my resume into something that resembled a media expert. But after I started detailing all the jobs I did for my media-based clients, it started to seem somewhat impressive. Though I looked at myself just as a tech support operator, in reality I helped my clients build and implement a content management system. This type of system is the number-one tool companies use to publish content to their Website. Although my role seemed insignificant at the time, in hindsight, I was their lifeline for a crucial part of their business. I didn't fully comprehend how important my work was to others. I was not only experienced but instrumental to their success. Looking at my work with this kind of mindset helped put all my daily tasks that seemed boring and rote at the time appear as pretty remarkable and pivotal on my resume.

Once complete, I sent my handcrafted media resume to Rich, and he forwarded it on to his recruiter friend. Even though at first I felt that my media credentials were lacking, I now felt positive about them. Regardless of my credentials, it wasn't going to hurt me to submit my resume to see where it may lead. Rejection is some of the best learning experience one can get. Rich didn't know the pay scale of the job, if it was Agile-related or not, or if it was international. Regardless, a trusted friend's introduction is the preferred road to take for any job. And I had to admit that working for a media company seemed interesting, so why not gave it a try?

As it so happened, a few days later, Rich's friend called me for an interview. We met in person, and I explained my current situation and told him what I was looking for, which was a job within my career niche of international Agile software project management, with a caveat that I want to make more money than I do now. As always, I inflated my current income by ten grand and said I was currently making $95,000. Once again, I gave this threshold, figuring I could always accept a lower-paying job if it was the right fit. Also, there was the same risk anyone assumes when leaving a paycheck (even in a struggling company) for a new unknown job. Maybe the new job stinks worse than where I am currently. Maybe I'll get less vacation days. Or maybe my current job finds out I'm interviewing and decides instead of paying me more to make me happy, they reduce my pay (which would actually make me interview more, but whatever). These potential risks always add up to $10,000 for me. Although my deadline was quickly approaching to make six figures, I didn't hate my job so much that I would leave for the same amount of money and start over. I had to have an extra incentive.

The feedback I got from the recruiter wasn't exactly what I wanted to hear, but it was intriguing. The recruiter mostly worked in finance, filling spots on Wall Street in short-term contracts. These contracts were mostly hundreds of dollars an hour and working with number-crunching financial systems. As Wall Street was taking a beating during the down economy, he was looking to move into the media industry and trying to expand his recruiting business in a new market.

The media job he was trying to fill was for a software consultancy that had only one media client, and that client was ESPN. Now I perked up. ESPN was my dream situation bringing me back to my sports industry vertical I had earlier identified as a passion career. Instantly I imagined being able to talk sports all day at work and maybe I'd potentially get spare tickets to some sporting events and more. How perfect would that be? I also envisioned that, for the first time ever, a boss's use of sports analogies during meetings would be encouraged by all. And maybe we'd see some professional athletes come through the office and I could grill them on some of my off-the-wall sports theories. The job might be like *Moneyball*. Or those *SportsCenter* commercials. Either way, I was hooked. As enticing as it was, it came with one catch. It was just a six-month contract job with a potential, but no guarantee, to be hired on as a full-time employee. Also it wasn't exactly my niche as it wasn't internationally dispersed teams. And they weren't sure if they were going to use Agile or not as their software development process, but they wanted to hire someone with Agile certification just in case. So I had at least one thing working for me.

On top of that, working as a contractor, I would not have health insurance benefits, 401k options, and the other full-time employee perks and job security that come with having a full-time job. One major difference is that instead of being an employee who would usually have allotted two-weeks paid vacation and a handful of paid sick days off, I'm effectively treated like a business where any day I don't come to work is just an unpaid day for me. Calculating what you would be making on your days off makes your vacations much less enjoyable and your ailments that much more painful. Also being a "business" instead of an employee comes with a whole additional level of personal responsibility: invoicing and billing for your hours, negotiating contract terms every six to 12 months, and treating your boss like you would a client (the usual boss-employee relationship plus more ass-kissing). On the other hand, your overtime and weekend hours are billable, potentially at a higher rate, while your salaried coworkers are not being paid a dime more. Depending on your line of work, that can be the best perk of all.

If you know a company inside and out but can't secure a full-time position, then

Subversive Job Tip

reach out to a decision-maker in the company via LinkedIn and offer a partnership. Instead of being a job-seeker, you are now perceived as an equal, and an entrepreneurial one at that. Mention you understand the needs of the company and that you are thinking of building your own business to assist in solving a specific problem you know they have. Inquire if they would be open for a lunch to pick their brain about how best to solve this problem of theirs. You come out of it with a lunch date, possibly a full-time or contract job, or better yet, a solid business plan. Bonus Points: If rejected, ask for referrals to others of his or her caliber. If necessary, name drop a few you'd like to meet. You now are setting up a situation of being introduced by a bigwig to another bigwig. This also works if the lunch date goes well, too.

Also, as a contractor I would have to always be mentally prepared for the fact that I'd possibly have to do another job hunt again in six months. It would be too precarious to bank on a full-time job being available once my contract concluded. As financially risky as I am at times, I always prefer a steady income. My unemployment days of depression flashed before my eyes and the recruiter sensed me becoming hesitant. Thinking through all of these pros and cons of contracting sort of befuddled me. Not being sure how to respond to the recruiter's description of this once-in-a-lifetime position, I told him I'd have to think about it and I'd get back to him.

The recruiter did a few back-of-the-envelope calculations to help persuade me into accepting. I could tell he didn't know the going rate for a media-based contractor; he worked purely in finance up until this point. He was used to paying similar positions huge sums of money. I didn't know the current rate either, as contracting was fairly new to me. And he also knew this was my first official entry into media, regardless of the experience detailed on my resume. Then he said, "I understand you don't want to leave the safety of your current job for a six-month contract gig. To make up for the loss of health insurance and more, I'll get you compensated enough so you could do those things out of pocket. I'll also reduce the cut I take, so you can get more money per hour. I'm hoping to get my foot in the door in the media world here, so I'm willing to work with you and work for less. If you were to make $95 an hour, would that be acceptable to you?"

Holy shit balls! The quickest way to guesstimate hourly figures into a salary is to double it. So if you are making $20 an hour, then that would be effectively making close to $40,000 a year. With $95/hour, I calculated in my head that I would be making $190,000 a year! This contract would bring in $95,000 in six-months, it was unbelievable. I'm sure my eyes were screaming "Yes, yes, yes!" but I tried to be as cool as possible, and I shrugged and said "Sure, that would work." I was pretty sure this was more than it should pay, but I wasn't going to talk him down. I also couldn't believe such an average dude who a year ago was on unemployment could now get paid so much. I figured there had to be a catch, and I started plowing through worst case scenarios. The worst I could come up with was not getting hired full-time at the end of the contract. I would not be able to get unemployment checks, as those only go to full-time employees, not contractors. And then I pictured what would happen if I couldn't find a job six months after my contract ended. Identifying my worst case scenario made the decision easy. Working for six months as a contractor and then not working at all for six months after that would still make me $10,000 more than staying at my current job for twelve months. At the speed everything was going, I was hopeful it wouldn't take me six months to find another job. Everyone has a price, and my price apparently was $95 an hour. Of course I was going to take the job if it was offered to me.

I wanted this job so bad I even went shopping for a new wardrobe. (Cue montage!) Daddy needed a new pair of shoes—and a tie, and slacks, and button down shirt. After six lengthy interviews during a span of six long weeks of anxious desire, I finally got offered the job of a lifetime. To make it sweeter, the offer came on the exact day of the deadline I had set for myself to reach a six-figure income! It was all a bit serendipitous. Ol' Buck Greenback had heard my prayer. I didn't consider this job as reaching my goal of six-figure salary though, as it was a contracting gig and not a full-time position. However, I had no problem putting my pursuit of that on hold for six months to take the big bucks, and the risks with it, for now. A six-month hiccup in my goal was reasonable I concluded, as the money was so great. I figured I'd pursue the full-time salary portion once this stint was over. Not a bad place to be in.

Like Scrooge McDuck, I was going to be swimming in cash now, but I wasn't feeling completely comfortable. I now had to prove myself to my friend Rich, his recruiter friend, ESPN, and most importantly, the consultancy that hired me that I was worth such a large amount of money. I also had to begin to mentally prepare my days as a contractor instead of an employee. I also felt pressure to perform to this newly obscene pay grade. Yes, that's me complaining about this awesome jolt to my life. I'm like Ben Franklin complaining about his key shocking him. But I was up for the task. I had no choice but do everything possible to wow them.

I put in my two-week notice at my current gig as an Application Manager. My impending departure wasn't much surprise to Don, who knew I was looking to get out as soon as Joanna left for more money too. The company tried its best to keep me with their recent raise and reimbursement, and that made me feel good. I felt validated and appreciated by those actions and made the decision that much harder. I simply had no choice but to move on if I wanted greener pastures—green being the color of money, pastures being where money grows, obviously. I told him I'd regret saying no to working with my dream company ESPN, and they understood that too and wished me luck.

Working in media was a completely new beast. My first three months were eye-opening. I had to learn a whole new terminology, business workflows, and more. I was constantly learning new things, asking non-stop questions, and trying to retain as much of it as I could. I love jobs like this; it makes the day go by quickly. I can feel myself growing as an employee, which means I'm building a bigger arsenal for my resume. New skills mean new opportunities, so I never pass down the chance to learn something new. I thought that maybe a media-based project manager expert was an even narrower niche I could create for myself moving forward. Being in media might open up bigger doors, just like working in marketing opened up a door to my last gig.

After working 40 hours a week for the first five months, I had torpedoed my way back to financial security. I felt like a new man, on strong footing and with the confidence to take on the world. I had indeed talked a lot of sports during that time period and even got complimentary front row seats to the Mets game. It was as exciting as I anticipated, but also more work than I imagined. Just learning the lingo of the industry was a full-time job on top of my other duties, but I found a way to produce positive results. It was the perfect career move at the right time.

As my contract was ending shortly, I inquired if the potential full-time position was still an option for me. In contract gigs like this, it comes down to budgeting. Sometimes they have it in a budget for a full-time position, sometimes they have a budget to award you another six-month contract, and sometimes they've just run out of money in the budget and you are on your way. It's really out of your control and it's best to ask early and often of their plans for you down the road.

The reply I got back from my full-time job inquiry was they would love to keep me onboard, but all they had available was a junior position in another state. I took that as "we like you, but you're too damn expensive and we've about busted the budget." Fair enough, I felt like I was overpaid for what I was doing anyway. They could easily get someone much cheaper to finish the remaining work (or employ someone with much more expertise than me for the same rate). I made the most of it while I was there, and I still had a month of hard work ahead of me. As much as I would have loved being at ESPN full-time, I was not ready to relocate the family for a pay cut. Based on the flurry of activity I had last time I was on the job market, I knew there would be plenty of other options out there for me. I just had to do the recruiter rodeo once again. Luckily, I had a month to find something before I was paycheck-less again.

You never know where your **Subversive Job** next lead will come from. A ca- **Search 101** sual conversation over dinner totally catapulted my career and income into a different stratosphere. I highly recommend letting people know what you are up to career-wise, especially as you hit big milestones, earn promotions, or increase your credentials. I'd even mention it on your status on Facebook and Twitter. Do you not know what so many of your friends do for a living? They probably don't know what you do either. Both parties are doing themselves a disfavor by not advertising their recent accomplishments and not using the social networks you already check daily to their advantage. (The Facebook app BranchOut can help you with this. InTheDoor.com is a good tool too.) I'd even offer a referral fee to my friends. Propose $150 to any of your friends or family that can make an introduction that leads to a job offer you want. This also works if you are unemployed. You might not have the money now, but sharing some of that first paycheck shouldn't be a problem. Somebody out there probably has an aunt, ex-boss, or dog walker who knows of someone looking for someone that does exactly what you do. And they may pay obscenely more. So announce your workplace success and update others on your progress. Be proud of what you have earned with your hard work. It's not bragging if it's hard fought and impressive. And if they are truly your friends, you'll get their support no matter what you are sharing. It all boils down to one thing: you are broadening your network by sharing your career progress, and that might just lead you to a few remarkable job leads. It doesn't hurt to try.

My first instinct when hearing about the job was I didn't have media experience. What would have happened if I didn't follow up and see what this job entailed? Now imagine how many opportunities you may have passed up because you didn't spend 30 minutes to tweak a resume? Those 30 minutes more than doubled my pay. I'd gladly do it again and again for all future job offers. Even if you feel like you aren't a perfect fit, throw your hat into the ring and apply anyway. You may be a better fit than you think you are. If you are an outsider and still get offered the job, take learning new skills, new terminology, and new processes as a benefit, not a chore. Each of these things is potentially a new feather in your expertise hat.

Sometimes a special opportunity trumps your goals, sometimes the money will. But the thing to remember is to make these unique scenarios temporary, not the standard. If you are constantly jumping around then you are hurting your career progression. It made more sense for me to work for six months for top pay than to stay where I was and work for twelve months. This slight detour made financial sense and didn't significantly impact my career goals. There was even a chance that this new market would enhance my employability down the road as I was now working with a big-name client like ESPN. I took it as a challenge to prove to others I was worth my pay and gave it my all, and I'm glad I did.

A contractor is synonymous with a freelancer. Basically you work for yourself via contracts. You don't need a special business license or business name to do this type of work; you can do it all under your name and Social Security number. There are a few added wrinkles to invoicing and billing your company to get your pay, but usually the HR department can walk you through those steps if you have never done it before. So yes, it will require a slightly more cerebral approach to your work when you are being treated as a business, rather than an employee, but not so much that it should interfere with your work. You'll also miss out on some employer benefits and some stability of income, but you may gain in some tax benefits. You can write off some monthly expenses like a home office, your mobile phone, and gas for your car. Depending on the work, you can many times create your own schedule, work from home, or other benefits. Contractors can also quickly gain a lot of industry knowledge working on a variety of projects among different clients. With this experience, it makes identifying an enjoyable career niche that much easier.

What You Can Do Today

Being a contractor is not just a great way to earn a huge hourly rate, but it's also a way to try out different occupations or quickly gain experience in fields you may be lacking. In short, you are working for you. You are your own boss; you sign a contract and you get to work. The rest is on you to deal with and handle, including collecting paychecks and making sure you are sticking to the agreed contract. If you are not sure how to even start as a contractor or freelancer, there are tons of resources out there that can be found with a quick Google search.

I've found the quickest way to get started as a contractor to try out new occupations is on freelance Websites like TaskRabbit.com, Odesk.com, and Elance.com. You create a free resume-like profile and you bid on jobs. At the completion of jobs you get feedback, which serves as your contractor reputation. People live and die by these feedbacks, as they really make you stand out. You may have to work a couple of freebies to just get a few positive scores on your profile before you start charging a more appropriate rate.

When freelancing online, you are competing with a global market, so don't approach it as a place to replace your income (unless you have none). You will most likely be competing with someone in a different country willing to work for much less. It's okay; some people are looking for the best fit rather than the best price, and you will eventually find a way to get a gig. If your intentions are to test out new types of employment, it can't get any better. You can work for cheap on a short-term or long-term project (some only last one day) and there are openings for most skilled occupations that can be completed online or from home. In the chance that this freelancing confirms a new occupation as the right fit for you, then you really win big as you have already earned your first professional experience in your new career! You are working for yourself and you already have a customer referral. These are big scores that will propel you into any new career.

If you are lacking experience and need to make up ground, this is the fastest way to do it too. Many times, commissioned work online can be done on your schedule: late in the evening, lunch breaks, and other off-hour times. Yes, you are now working two jobs, but it is no different than taking night or weekend classes for someone who is lacking in education. Ramping up in the off-hours works just as well for experience-seekers as it does for education-seekers. You are working hard in the short term to benefit you in the long term. But keep your day job responsibilities quiet to your online clients; no one wants to hire someone who is doing other work on the side. If you are doing a good job, they won't notice. There is no need to share this information.

On the other hand, if you aren't interested in being a contractor, these sites can earn you praise at your current job by allowing you to pitch money-saving ideas to your boss. At three different positions I've had, I pitched a scheme to upper management and have gotten it approved to earn myself many compliments from those that matter. You start by identifying repetitive tasks being done by some of the most highly skilled and highly paid people in your office. Hopefully many of these tasks are your own. These can be data entry tasks, spreadsheet building, list making, e-mail grooming, canned responses, and more. If you spend an hour every day doing the same thing that a well-trained monkey could do, those are the tasks I'm talking about. I imagine you hate these daily or weekly soul-crushing tasks, and so did someone else at some point until they passed them on to you. These tasks are usually the ones you think about when you say "I hate my job." I have always finagled my way out of doing them while putting myself in good-standing with upper management, and I'll tell you how.

Your company should have your big salary guys be doing important tasks, not menial tasks. First thing you do is find contractors on TaskRabbit.com, Elance.com, or Odesk.com that would be willing to do your same repetitive tasks at a much lower price. Sometimes they work in a different time region which could work to your advantage. If that's the case, then you can send them tasks when you leave the office just as the contractor is starting his work day. Then he completes the work and submits back to you just as you're beginning your work day the next morning. Not only have you just identified a way to save money, but also you are more efficient at the same time.

If you can't identify any of your own tasks to outsource, then do it for others in the office. The more skilled or higher paid the person, the better. Then you pitch your boss the following, preferably in person:

I really want to focus on being the best [insert your job title] that I can be. I feel like my skills are not being used in the most effective way possible because I waste [insert time spent] a day doing [insert mundane task]. I know we don't have anyone else to do it, but you're paying an expert like me [insert hourly rate] to do this task. I know my expertise will better serve the company if I could be doing [insert career building task] instead.

I would like to propose a solution. We outsource this task, and I'll manage all the outsourced contractors. It's not additional work for you, and it will allow me to focus squarely on my expertise. I've already found someone that can do this task for [insert low rate] and have it done by 9:00 a.m. every day. She could also do [colleague's mundane task] for the same price. In the long run, it will save the company money, increase efficiency, and your most talented employees are focusing on higher-skilled tasks and not getting paid to do something a less capable person can handle.

It would only cost us [insert low price] to do a two-week trial. Can we give it a try starting Monday?

With this pitch, you are now the golden boy or girl of the office. You just identified a huge and expensive problem, provided a solution, and took ownership of its implementation. How could they say no? How could they not love you? With this move you get to do more career-progressing work, earn experience managing remote teams, eliminate a soul-crushing task, and receive kudos from upper management and from your overworked colleagues. You are now considered a leader and a valued employee. No doubt this will go a long way in your annual salary review.

And why does it work? Because your boss is a busy person and doesn't have time to think about new problems or solutions. You have put him or her in position to say "yes" or "no." And these are the easiest questions to get approved. A well-delivered proposal makes earning a yes that much easier.

Salary Science

When you are working for yourself, it's important to take as much time as necessary to get your life in order. If your life is a wreck, I imagine the "business" you are portraying is also in need of some serious work. Your mental and physical health plays a big role in how you perform in your job. A relaxed, happy worker is a good worker. Too much stress will affect the quality of your performance and will eventually compromise your wealth. Salaried workers should take heed of this advice too, considering a Harris Interactive survey[1] found salaried Americans on average don't use about 70 percent of their vacation days. How can anyone, salaried or a contractor, have a clear mind and do a good job if they work 24-7?

Also take the time to exercise, as it's known to boost mental function and improve your mood. A Penn State study[2] found the more active you are, the more likely you will show signs of excitement and enthusiasm. And I know plenty of people's moods at work that could use some uplifting. Karolinska Institute[3] did a study and found that professional Swedish soccer players test above average in creative problem solving, multi-tasking, and working memory. The more skilled they were at soccer, the higher they tested. So yes, exercise can make you smarter too.

For you non–Swedish professional soccer players, a Dartmouth study[4] found that a daily brisk walk alone can increase your cognitive ability. The study suggests that the regularity of exercise is what is important, not the intensity. Would you walk a mile a day for a 9 percent increase in your salary? I imagine you would, that's one hell of a bonus. This is good news considering A Journal of Labor Research study[5] found that those who exercise regularly indeed average a 9 percent higher salary than those who don't.

If you aren't willing to exercise, at least quit smoking. A tobacco study[6] by Ohio State has found that a non-smoker's net worth is usually double that of a heavy smoker, and even 50 percent higher than that of light smokers. I would suggest replacing the vice of cigarettes with the vice of alcohol. A Journal of Labor Research report[7] found that drinkers earn 10–14 percent more than teetotalers. Abstaining may save your money from high bar tabs, but may keep you from earning higher salaries. For men needing an extra incentive to go out, the following stat is sure to make you happy. Men that visit a bar at least once a month end up earning 7 percent more than those who don't go at all. The theory is that drinkers have a higher social capital that can be leveraged in business situations. Bar-goers are presented with more networking opportunities, usually have higher social skills, and are likely to talk more personally with clients and coworkers at a bar than in an office environment. So if you ever run out of reasons to drink, now you know it'll make you richer!

8

Recruiter Rodeo

Money is better than poverty, if only
for financial reasons.

—Woody Allen

I was excited to be on the job market again. It's funny
to say, but I've started to enjoy it. Eighteen months ago
I was collecting unemployment checks and swearing
at inanimate objects, now I'm genuinely giddy about
being on the job hunt once more. All the back and
forth with recruiters, picturing all the different possible lives for myself in new work environments, and
calculating every move to increase my salary has gotten
to be really fun. To make it even more interesting this
time around, I was quickly learning I had opened up a
whole new world of media-based job opportunities. My
newly minted ESPN experience was now added to the
top of my online resume, and it was getting a lot of attention. It was clear that at the moment there were very

few software project managers with media experience on the job market. But I was also getting attention in other industries too, ranging from insurance, publishing, marketing, and more. It seemed my Agile software niche had made me an in-demand hire across many industries.

It was also easier job hunting this time around, because I now had experience in "the game" played with recruiters. Some recruiters work in-house for one company, some recruiters work with various companies, and most have a focus on specific job roles or industries. Because of this, recruiters get paid in a variety of ways. Some of them get a flat fee, like a referral fee, if someone they recommend eventually gets hired. Other types of recruiters get a bonus for bringing you in at a cheaper rate, and they try to hammer you down to a lower salary. Depending on the job and where you are in your career, they can be your worst enemy. Of course, employers look at them as an ally, even though they usually result in hiring unconfident workers who end up unhappy for being underpaid. But at the end of the day recruiters are your ally as they solely work to fill their job listings. You just may be one of those hand-picked to fill the next job.

The beauty of recruiters is they can handle all the potentially uncomfortable talks for you. It's much easier for a recruiter to call your potential new boss 10 minutes after an interview and ask him how it went. Obviously if I did that as an interviewee, I would instantly be dismissed as a lunatic and rightfully so. If a recruiter does it, he's just doing his job. Recruiters can also ask pressing questions you may not feel comfortable asking. They can inquire on your behalf when a final decision will be made, if there is room to pay you more, how many other people are also interviewing for the same position, and anything else that crosses your mind. If recruiters are one thing, it is that they are slick. They can smooth talk, wheel and deal, and know how to lay on the charm when necessary. If dealing with these types of wheeler-dealers seems a bit overwhelming, don't fret. They are there to assist and give you very direct advice, usually when you need it the most. Hell, a good way to make the process seem exciting is to just picture a recruiter as your Hollywood agent and any job interviews he gets you as an audition for a blockbuster movie. But then don't go full Hollywood and blame your lack of a career on a crappy agent who doesn't return your phone calls.

The best recruiters are the flat fee recruiters or those that get paid a percentage of your salary, which is then paid by the company. I've never experienced a recruiter that takes money from your paycheck, so that shouldn't be a worry. The ones that get paid a percentage of your salary are ideal partners, as they get paid more if they get you paid more. If a recruiter asks for a hiring fee, introduction fee, or any adjective followed by the word "fee" then they are not legit. Never pay a recruiter anything. They always get paid by the company that hires you. You can ask upfront how the recruiter gets paid when you talk to one, and hope they tell you the truth, but you can also easily weed out the bad ones by having a game plan, a strong USP, and a commitment to a salary goal when you make first contact. A legit recruiter will take that information and get to work. A rogue one will follow up by asking you for a payment.

A good place to meet recruiters is at networking events. Recruiters usually concentrate in niche industries such as marketing, insurance, medical, and a myriad others. The best recruiters have a large pool of top-shelf applicants within a certain knowledge base and then have an equally large base of impressive hiring managers and companies looking for that same skill set. Really motivated recruiters then attend their industry-specific events, seminars, and conferences to hunt for more talented applicants and companies hiring now or in the future. You should be attending these events anyway to learn about what's happening in your chosen field, but meeting recruiters while you're there is also a nice bonus, especially if you can appear as an expert in your field.

But if you really want to flip the script and expedite the process of meeting recruiters, I'd recommend attending a conference, seminar, or event targeting the recruiting industry. If you show up with a ton of mini-resumes, shake a lot of hands, and make yourself memorable as the only job hunter at a recruiter-only event, I promise that if doors don't open for you, your network will expand at least tenfold. With that kind of networking boost, you'll reap benefits quickly. But remember, it's not just showing up at these events; you have to be an excellent salesman too. Recruiters of all people know how to sell, so you have your work cut out for you.

Look sharp when meeting a recruiter. It's no different than if you were going on a job interview. First impression is key here. In a down economy, recruiters are overwhelmed with unemployed applicants. There are just too many to remember and to place. They will be looking for a reason to dismiss you as fast as possible, as they only want to be associated with the crème de la crème. Make eye contact, be confident, and have a prepared elevator pitch to grab a recruiter's attention (it should be similar to the USP you identified for yourself already). That way, recruiters can quickly gauge if they should invest in learning more about you or not. If a conversation goes well, then pull out a pen and some pre-printed business cards that have your LinkedIn URL and text that reads, "Hi, I'm [your name]. We met at [blank] and we talked [blank]." Fill it out quickly and slip it to the recruiter. If a conversation doesn't go well, don't fret—it gives you more time to find someone else.

When talking to recruiters, it is important to make your career demands known early and upfront, otherwise you are shooting yourself in the foot. Without a plan, recruiters may steer you into something that is not the correct fit and it will end up wasting everyone's time. Or even worse, a recruiter will take your lack of priorities as desperation, and no one is excited about someone who is willing to take any ol' job in the world (even if you are). As I said before, I recommend always saying you are making $10,000 more than you currently do (they have no way of confirming), and then saying you're looking for jobs that are $5,000 more on top of that. For the unemployed, say you are currently contracting or freelancing, and are looking for a full-time job. Remember, it's in the recruiter's best interest to supply qualified applicants with a good work record, so don't go overboard or they won't even submit your resume. Most likely an offer will come in slightly below whatever you say. I believe you should slowly prove yourself worthy at $10,000 to $15,000 salary increments; it will help build confidence and prepare you for the big bucks later on. A pay increase of more than that at a time will just set you up for failure, and that's never a good place to be in. Occasionally, a new job will reference check your current salary or ask to supply current pay stubs, so don't embellish too much. Coming up $10,000 short is usually acceptable as it could be intangible payments such as an upcoming bonus, promised promotion, or even extra vacation days that you have earned. As long as you can safely value an extra $10,000 from your current situation and explain it to your new job when pressed, then you are in the clear.

You'll meet recruiters from all walks of life, and they all have access to different listings, some posted publicly and some not. Because of this, it's good to have as many recruiters as possible working on your behalf during your job hunt. You should constantly be trying to find new recruiters and checking in with the ones you do have. I've found a lot of recruiters online. They swarm LinkedIn like it's a honeycomb of crack—which, based on the amount of endorphins it probably generates for them, it is. I find recruiters on my friend's profiles and ask for e-mail introductions, or I reach out to them directly in a private message. Sometimes, they come find me. The same happens on Twitter. All I do is a simple search of "job" and "NYC" or browse TwitJobSearch.com. Most of the results are job listings posted by recruiters. A quick Twitter follow of that person, a 140-character introduction, and I'm now part of this person's network in a matter of seconds. It doesn't take much effort to find recruiters online, even for agoraphobes, technophobes, or phobophobes. As long as you have a great USP or strong career bio on your online profile, the rest should fall in place.

And yes, sometimes it takes a year or two before I ever hear back from a recruiter. The majority of recruiters forget about you after a couple weeks unless they have something right at that moment that is a good fit. But they will keep your resume in their own internal database for a potential gig down the road. It is important to understand this: recruiters don't read your resume and then go off and find you a job. They get assigned a job listing, and then they go off and try to find the best person for that job. It may take months before they reach out to you as their current job listings may be completely unrelated to what you do. Yes, some recruiters are slimy used-car-dealer types and others are like your best friend (not slimy and no car). All in all, a recruiter does not get paid if he can't find a qualified employee to fill an open position. In the meantime, do your best to appear as a qualified employee.

Subversive Job Tip

If you can't find a job for yourself, connect others instead. Following leads and postings of recruiters and hiring managers and then introducing them to people you think would make a great fit greatly increases your social capital. Sometimes recruiters offer referral fees up to $1,500 if you recommend someone they need who gets hired. This will open up doors for you on both sides of the equation: the recruiter may look to repay you with an introduction of his own and the newly hired friend can help you get a foot in the door at this new company. Bonus Points: Build a network of referral-paying recruiters by just e-mailing them and letting them know you get a lot of impressive resumes that you occasionally like to pass on. Then pay $20 to post a generic job listing online to generate a whole slew of leads that you can then send to the recruiter. It's not only a great networking opportunity, but potentially a very lucrative side gig.

Because recruiters like to focus in certain careers, I've found it works best when they find me via my public resume on niche career-listing Websites. If your resume has been thoroughly A/B tested like mine now has, be prepared for an onslaught of contact once you upload to a job-listing site.

With my new media resume, I was doing this as I hit the job market scene full force. Just like in dating, where the taken people always seem the most attractive, the same goes with job hunting. You are in higher demand if you are currently employed. If possible, always try to start your hunt prior to contracts ending, being fired or laid off, or even quitting. Worst case scenario, find work freelancing online, even if it is working for free, just so you can say you are currently employed. Spin it positively by saying you are freelancing to earn more experience in your field quickly. This is so much better than being billed as a desperate job seeker, especially when salary negotiations will soon be occurring.

When I started my job search, each recruiter was blown away that I was making $95 an hour. I had since learned the peak market rate for my position was around $65 an hour. I knew it was insane too, but this first impression set up that I was obviously qualified for something north of $100,000. I obviously didn't show my cards and agree I was being overpaid, but I knew I wasn't going to find a matching salary and shared my realistic expectations with the recruiters.

Within a few weeks, I received many media-related interviews, now that my LinkedIn profile was updated with my recent ESPN experience. Some of these interviews were to jobs that were an hour away or more. These paid up to $130,000, but it didn't fit my specified criteria of being in New York City. Other jobs were for similar contracting gigs like the one that I was just wrapping up, lasting six or 12 months and paying the still-impressive rate of $65 an hour. These were located close-by too, but I was now looking for a long-term fit at a salaried position. I wanted to settle down at a place for a few years and really become part of a company. Some of the negative feedback I got the last job hunting session was that my resume had too many six and 12 month stints on it. This could paint me as a flight risk and not worth the risk in hiring and training for a full-time position. It was a valid assumption, and I knew long-term employment had to be my next move to remove this question mark on my resume.

As I had just one month left in my contract at ESPN, I also gave myself one month of sticking to my original career wish list of doing Agile project management in New York City at an international company. Top dollar wasn't the end game for me anymore; I wanted the perfect long-term fit. It became my new goal. It's always good to reevaluate your goals if you find they are no longer fitting your most urgent needs. I was financially secure enough now thanks to the contracting gig that money was no longer the main issue. Luckily I was now in a position to say that an extra $10,000 wasn't going to change my life. With this newfound financial security, I said no for now to anything not matching my desired criteria. Once my current contract ended (along with my ridiculously high paychecks), then I would probably reconsider my demands fairly quickly.

Once again, confidence was running high. (Things always seem to work better than expected when I feel good about myself.) I was in contact with about 15 different recruiters, some I've worked with before, some who I found online, and others who found me online. On top of that, I was searching and applying to job listings directly with companies on my own. The synergy of all that I've done up to this point from my online branding, my fully tweaked resume, and the confidence of being an expert in a tiny niche paid off for me as I was able to book three in-person interviews for the following week.

A recruiter arranged one of the interviews at a media company, another recruiter arranged an interview at a publishing company, and I had even booked myself an interview through my resume-sniping at another publishing company, but it did have an international team and offices all around the world. This was something I liked and wanted to get back into. The direction I chose now would probably set the path for my career from here on out.

All three jobs fit my career preferences on location and all of them required Agile software knowledge and experience. However, two of the jobs stood out more than the third one. The scheduling for all the interviews was rough, as my interviews were happening in mid-December. This meant many of the people I had to meet with were about to leave town for the holidays. To help with scheduling, I quickly eliminated the media job opportunity that I had found for myself. It would have had me working on a major publication's Website and accompanying apps using all the latest technologies and gadgets. It would be an exciting place to work, no doubt. However, after a marathon six-hour interview session, I left thinking it wasn't the ideal fit. When they invited me back for one more day of interviews I let them know that this job wasn't for me. I anticipated much longer hours and potentially less pay here than the other two were going to have. Also, I knew if I wasn't excited about it right off the bat that my performance would suffer and probably not be beneficial to the company or to me. The other two potential job opportunities were a much better fit in the long run and I didn't want to compromise on my next career move so early on in the job hunt. (In hindsight, maybe confidence was running a little too high for me to be eliminating jobs I wasn't even being offered yet.)

The recruiters for the two remaining opportunities were doing everything they could for me to meet with the right people before the Christmas holidays. Time was of the essence, as each position had a start date of the first week of January. Because it was mid-December, I knew a) there wasn't time for them to be interviewing multiple people for this position which possibly made me the only candidate, and b) they would have to make a decision quickly in order to get someone onboard by the new year. The conversations I had with the recruiters confirmed this. This let me know that I was in the driver's seat negotiation-wise, and if offered a job, I would definitely have some leverage when it came time to discuss compensation.

I could feel that I was now very close to not only reaching my new long-term career goal with a perfect fit, but also my six-figure salary goal that I had set for myself 18-months earlier. Achieving both was now possibly just a few weeks away. But of course, I had to ace these interviews first or nothing was going to happen. Having gone on so many interviews within the past year and a half, they had become second nature. This added bonus made me more relaxed and confident, both huge advantages during the interview process. I learned to ask as many questions as they asked me. This not only showed that I really cared about the job, but it made the interviewer comfortable too. If I got them talking about themselves and the company for half the interview, then it would mean less time for me to screw it up. (Also when people talk about themselves a lot they usually leave with a higher impression of you.) So I did a lot of research on both companies and their competitors, and came prepared with a lot of questions.

I'm not sure when this became standard in the corporate world, but I held another marathon all-day interview session with the first company which I'll call company A. I met nine different people during five hours. It was a bit overwhelming. One noteworthy part of the process was that the recruiter who set me up on this interview told me not to talk money at all. He wanted to handle all compensation talks if an offer came in. I had previously told him I was looking for something near $95,000, so I knew the job paid at least close to that. Of course, one of the first questions I was asked while interviewing at Company A was what my salary expectations were. I let them know the recruiter instructed me not to talk numbers and they obliged. This act eliminated the most awkward and most sensitive part of the interview process, making me even more comfortable.

At one point I couldn't grasp why I had to interview with one of the people I was set up with, so I inquired if we would potentially be working together. She didn't think we would and didn't really know why she was interviewing me either. It may be one of those vetting processes where as long as everyone agrees an applicant was safe, no one is singularly responsible for hiring a bad seed. Or most likely, they needed to fill 30 minutes before I had to meet with the next person, someone who I would be working directly with. She and I also speculated the person I really needed to meet had already left for vacation. So I took the opportunity to ask a lot of questions to gauge the work/life balance of the company and to really try to paint a picture of the office environment that I would maybe be a part of soon. What I heard from her was really impressive. It seemed like most of the people I talked to had worked there for at least five years, so that told me the company must be doing something right. She herself had been there six years. It definitely wasn't like the start-up I was in with Joanna where we had a rotating door of coworkers.

After learning this nice tidbit, I went off and interviewed with another three more people. By the end of it, I was exhausted. I felt I had done above-average through each interview and with such a long day I left with a good handle of what I would be getting myself into if I worked there. And from what I learned, this job sounded ideal. It wasn't in the media industry; however, I wasn't sure I wanted to make that a permanent career move. It did have international teams and offices, and I would occasionally get to travel around the world as part of my job duties. That seemed like a great perk to me. The work environment didn't seem like a pressure cooker; everyone seemed relatively relaxed and, judging the body language of those in the cubicles around the office, in good spirits. If they offered me the job, even if the salary was below $95,000, I knew I would accept it. It was exactly what I was looking for in a long-term position.

As Christmas was now only three days away, I expected a quick answer on whether a job offer for Company A was forthcoming or not. The recruiter had actually called my potential boss 10 minutes after I was done with all my interviews to get the full scoop. He then let me know he expected an offer to come in the next day. As I was leaving for my third-round interview the following morning for Company B, the recruiter called me with the expected great news. He reminded me of stability of Company A, he preached the benefits and health insurance package, and then he talked about the salary. The salary is always the juiciest news. And the juice here was that the job paid $98,000! Whoa ho, Jesus H. Paycheck! I was floored and overjoyed. I was going to land a great long-term position, and while at it, I had almost reached my goal of six-figures too. It had been a long year and a half, and finally it all paid off. It was shy of the magical $100,000 threshold, but again, that wasn't my main goal at this point. Plus, I'm sure I could find a way to finagle $2,000 during the course of the year using my previous workplace treasure hunting techniques. In the meantime, I was ecstatic that all my work resume-testing, certificate getting, networking, re-branding, and niche-making had paid off in full. This time I wasn't going to complain about how nice life was treating me. Goal setting, optimism, and dedicated focus had propelled me to almost reaching two huge career goals at one time. I was indeed on cloud nine; just as I expected I would be so many months earlier when I made it a mission to rebuild a new corporate life for myself.

The offer was obviously impressive, and because I was just about to start my next interview at Company B, I didn't want to give an official acceptance to Company A just yet. Although I wasn't officially complaining, I figured I could at least see if I could get a little bit more out of the offer. I reminded myself with such a tight deadline on the start date that I did have some leverage here and it was a ripe opportunity to be a bit subversive once more. I knew the recruiter wouldn't get paid unless I accepted the job, so why not let him earn his pay—he wanted to control the money talks, after all.

I've learned through the years the first offer at any job is rarely the only offer. Most bosses expect you to negotiate so they purposely give you a lower first offer to begin with, but it's on you to start the negotiations. Don't ever just say "Yes, when do I start?" So instead of telling the recruiter I was on my way to another interview, I told him I already had a competing offer on the table, and that I needed some time to think both offers over.

Obviously, as I was still interviewing I didn't exactly have another job offer on the table. The recruiter that had gotten me interviews at Company B was getting positive feedback from the people that I had already interviewed with and he told me I was indeed the only person they were interviewing for the position. They just couldn't officially give me an offer until I met with the last two higher ups, one who had unfortunately already started his winter vacation. So it was understood that after my interview today I would have to come back the first week of January to get one last official in-person interview and then I'd receive an official offer.

The recruiter of Company A was obviously saddened by this news, as his potential payday was now up in the air. Banking on his Christmas spirit (or more accurately Company A's Christmas spirit), I let him know I needed him to sweeten the pot for me, the "competing offer" I had was much better. I informed him that I prefered Company A's job more (I was equally pleased with both jobs), but the other job offered $15,000 more (wishful thinking) and more vacation days (blind optimism), and would he see if they could match that offer for me? I may have been getting greedy, but there is no harm in letting your potential employer with an offer on the table think that you are in high-demand. I would have never done this type of negotiation by myself, but if the recruiter could potentially get a better offer for me, then why not try? Realistically, I had no expectations for the first company to match the offer. I kept it to myself that I would still take the job even if the recruiter came back and said he couldn't do anything and the first offer remained the same.

It took about an hour for him to get back to me. As I was exiting my Company B interview, the recruiter called me back with an update. He let me know Company A didn't have it in the budget to match the imagined offer I gave them, but they could offer a better all-around package. Instead they countered with an extra week of vacation, I could work from home twice a week, and my starting salary could be bumped up to $105,000! I was officially into the six-figure threshold! Plus, the company said I could have a salary review at nine months instead of 12 months. The extra vacation and the work-from-home flexibility were worth more to me than the extra money, but of course I'll always take a higher salary too. This complete package blew me away. This proposal was great in many ways, and not just monetarily. The offer showed Company A was serious, they believed in investing in me as an employee, and they would do what they could to make me happy. It was clear now why everyone there stayed for years.

This was going to be a great move for my career, and an added bonus was that I had not only achieved, but exceeded my $100,000 milestone!

I accepted on the spot and informed Company B I didn't have time to wait until January for another interview; I had an exceptional offer on the table that I couldn't pass up. They understood and let me know to reach out if things didn't work out. I was going to be financially secure for a long time now and I couldn't wait to get started. I had officially and subversively gone from niche to rich and now I planned to stay that way. I gave myself a pep talk that I better not screw this one up—even if it makes for a good third book!

Subversive Job Search 101

Recruiters can be a great source of knowledge on gauging your worth. They look at hundreds of resumes and job listings every day and can quickly judge your employability and your salary range. They will let you know if you are asking too much, if you are lacking in skills, or if you are currently being overpaid. It's worth talking to a few recruiters at least once a year to know where you stand on the job market. Even if you have no plans to leave, you could possibly use the recruiter's feedback when it's time to negotiate a raise at your current job. Recruiters are excellent at pin-pointing your strengths and your weaknesses, and getting their feedback can be extremely useful.

Leverage recruiters as much as possible to do any dirty work for you. Have them handle the awkward money talks. Get them to ask the intrusive questions. Get them to anticipate your chance of being hired both before and after the interview. They are already doing this, as they have to figure out if they need to find other applicants or not. It doesn't hurt to request for the recruiters to share this information with you too. It's important to ask them why a job opening even exists. Are they trying to fill a job for someone who just left the company? If so, then they are probably in more of an urgent need to get the position filled. Is it a newly created position? It may mean someone is already doing the work and they just want to shed a few people's responsibilities, or it could mean the company is growing. Also figuring out why someone left could help you see your potential future. Maybe the person left because that is what she needed to do to advance her career. Maybe the job was underpaid. These are assumptions; every job is different, so ask many questions so you can make the best decision possible.

If you haven't heard from a recruiter in about three weeks, check back in. Maybe he can tell you that you are lacking some crucial skills, your niche is currently not hiring, or your demands are too specific or unreasonable. It's possible he's thrown your resume in the trash because your USP is unsellable or because you didn't make an outstanding first impression. Perhaps it's just not worth his time to let you know what skills you are lacking. Maybe he has 10 other applicants who are well-rounded experts to deal with instead. Knowing how you compare to the competition and knowing exactly what you want will help recruiters place you. Recruiters' reputations mean everything to earn repeat business from their clients, so they only want to send the best employees. They may invite you in for an interview to see how you stack up, and you need to take this interview as seriously as you would with an actual company. They can be your roadblock to employment as much as they are a gateway to employment. Make them like you. Otherwise, if they don't ignore you altogether, they may steer you into something that is just a good match for them. It's a fine balance to make sure your demands are realistic given the current market conditions, but also be pushing the envelope for as much money as possible.

If you are just starting out in your career, you may go after whatever position offers top dollar. It's a tough impulse to overcome, and occasionally it proves to be the correct move. If you appreciate vacation days, expected working hours, a flexible work schedule, and low stress levels, then it's usually advantageous to go for the job with more perks and a more relaxed work environment than one with high stress and high pay. As mentioned before, happiness goes a long way in being a productive worker.

When interviewing, ask as many questions as they ask you. A one-sided conversation comes off looking and feeling like an interrogation, rather than an interview.

A good back-and-forth rapport shows you are engaging, inquisitive, and interested in the company. By asking questions, you are demonstrating you are not going to just take any job, but the right job. If you are doing it right, sometimes they'll spend the whole time convincing you that you should work there, rather than the other way around. (This interview jujitsu is the holy grail of job hunts.) No matter what, if asked, always say you have another interview lined up at another company. You need to *appear* to be in demand, no matter the state of the economy, your excitement about the position, or desperation for a paycheck.

If you can't push off the money talks onto a recruiter, then come prepared for an answer to the dreaded questions regarding your expected salary. Try to deflect the question by saying "I'd like to see if I'm a good fit first. If so, then the salary numbers can be flexible. Can you explain more about the position and the company?" Or use the anchoring technique and say "Is a million dollars out of your budget? Ok, then I'd be looking in the $65,000 to $70,000 range." If you absolutely must provide a salary range then expect that the lowest number you mention is what you are going to get offered.

Joanna told me recently whenever she has her annual review she has a refrain in her head of "What would Alan do?" (I must admit, the phrase would look good on a plastic bracelet.) She's learned from our lunches that the company will approach all salary discussions as a business decision, and not a personal decision. Likewise, your response should also be based on a business decision and not a personal one. If you look at yourself as a business rather than an employee, then it's easy to conclude that asking for more is in the best interest of your company. With this approach and identifying having low social risks for asking for more, Joanna has now added an extra $10,000 to her salary during the past two years that otherwise would have been left on the table.

What You Can Do Today

If you are attending multiple career seminars and industry conferences and still have trouble making the right connections, then it is time to up the ante. As they say, go big or go home. The going-big way to be noticed is to create your own celebrity by throwing an industry networking event for yourself.

Do this by first contacting a local bar or restaurant and arrange a date for a special happy hour deal or finger-food special in exchange for bringing 25–50 people through the doors. Then after creating a flashy name like "Healthcare Happy Hour" or "Meatpackers Meet Up," pool everyone you know that is of a similar career background to attend your event. To boost the attendance, invite recent college graduates, former coworkers, and post flyers and ads around town and online. Once you feel confident that you'll have a decent turnout, reach out and personally invite recruiters of your industry to your event. Invite one recruiter for every 20 people you expect to be there. Be sure to invite recruiters from different recruiting firms, as recruiters from the same firm usually do not provide much of an advantage because they already share job listings and resumes with each other. The recruiters will feel honored, job hunters will be appreciative, and you will appear as a networker and go-getter to both. Just don't forget supplying name tags and absolutely avoid getting drunk.

If you are in a new town, you could maybe do what my brother-in-law did to increase his own presence quickly. He just reached out to all the top executives he wanted to meet to join him for a "Tech Happy Hour" at a local bar. They all RSVPed in the affirmative, as they all wanted a chance to meet the other executives in town too. With the big suits committing to attend the event, he was then able to lock-in a local law firm and an accounting firm to sponsor the event and cover the cost of food and drinks. On top of that, the lawyers and accountants were encouraged to invite their big name clients to join too. With a few weeks of work, my brother-in-law threw one super successful happy hour and instantly became the most connected person in a town that he had lived in for a little more than a year. The event proved so popular, it became a monthly event, and he was able to build his own consulting business around all his newly gained high-end contacts.

If you can't fathom throwing your own networking event, then the very least you can do is create a LinkedIn profile or edit the one you have to help you improve your career prospects or income. LinkedIn is the number-one tool for business professionals, and the best part is that it is free. It's so ubiquitous that you will appear suspicious (or at least very non-career focused) if you don't have an up-to-date profile. It's usually the first thing I check out when I am about to meet anyone in a business setting, and I assume they are doing the same.

Not only is LinkedIn beneficial in career advancement and networking once you have a job, it's an excellent tool for finding jobs too. Recruiters can easily review your resume, locate you, and submit job offers without even picking up the phone. You can also "follow" companies you admire or want to track. This can help you keep abreast of personnel changes or new job postings.

If you find yourself lost or unsure of your next career step, LinkedIn makes it easy to browse other people's profiles to see how your career compares with theirs. This is an excellent way to see the career advancement of people whose job you want, and then you can try to mimic his or her footsteps in your own career. Or better yet, contact that person directly and ask him or her about being a mentor or for some general career guidance. Trust me, they'll be flattered.

There is a bit of an art to creating a great-looking profile. Spending some time here goes a long way. Give yourself an hour, and it will pay huge dividends. A solid photo of you in something business casual is a great start, but you can get by with no photo as long as the rest is top-notch. I recommend treating your profile like a resume with clear and concise notes. Bullet points accompanying your measured success markers or key responsibilities are much better than paragraphs of text describing mundane details of your daily work load. Giving concrete examples of workplace successes is highly encouraged. The majority of recruiters will skim your profile, so make it easy for them to grab onto the good stuff.

I highly recommend joining a few groups or associations on your profile. Even if you absolutely cannot picture yourself attending a networking event on your own, that's completely cool. Joining a LinkedIn alumni group, or industry association group, requires no commitments of any kind and it's free. You never have to go to a meeting and you don't have to subscribe to their e-mails. When you join, it just puts the name of the association on your profile page. That's it. You are done. Now if I'm a hiring manager and I come to Bo Schmo's page (Joe's bean-counting brother), I can see that Bo is a member of The Cleveland Heights Accountants Group, CPA Association of Ohio, Accounting For Kids!, and the Annual Rustbelt Accounting Convention. Without knowing Bo, he at least looks like he loves talking about accounting based on his LinkedIn groups. I'd guess he regularly meets others like him, has a strong local and regional presence in the accounting community, and likes sharing his knowledge with children. I'd love to have this guy on my team; he seems like a solid and trustworthy hire! In reality, Bo was forced into his profession by his parents, he dreads going to work, he's done it too long to do anything else, and he's never participated in any of those groups' activities. Maybe I'll piece that all out of him in an interview, but at least he's getting an interview.

But Bo's twin Sally Schmo is also an accountant and is an active member of these same groups. Sally answers people's questions in the group's forums, takes time to private message her replies for when she needs to give more details, and regularly meets others for coffee or at meet-ups to learn more about how others are doing accounting. Consequently, Sally's profile page becomes loaded with professional recommendations, and she is highly revered within the Ohio accounting community. She's made herself a big fish in a relatively small pond. She'll easily find her way to a dream accounting position that pays top dollar; everyone knows Sally is the best. You know too, because all the other accountants have said so right there on her LinkedIn page! Which Schmo are you going to be?

Lastly, once your LinkedIn profile is up to snuff, I recommend the entry-level career Website OneDayOneJob. com. Their idea of using targeted Facebook ads is brilliant. On Facebook, all the ads you see in the columns are targeted ads. If you are seeing weight loss ads, teeth whitening ads, or wedding dress ads, it probably means you've just changed your relationship status from single to engaged. If you "like" a certain band or artist page, you'll probably start getting ads for similar musicians in the same genre. Have a good look at your Facebook ads now and figure out why you are receiving them. It's both interesting and freaky that it can all be tracked to your profile information or your recent activity. So use this technology to your advantage by making a personal ad to appear on the pages of employees of your specific company.

First, Google "Facebook ad coupons," and you can occasionally get a free coupon to get started. If it's not happening for you, then expect to spend about $50. Once you are ready to go, it'll take about 10 minutes to create your ad. Next, upload your headshot with a simple statement directly addressing the company you want to work for. For example, "Hi, I'm Lilly. I want to work for the Museum of Modern Art. Please see my resume attached so you can help me land my dream job." Now that your ad is done, Facebook will ask you on what pages you want this ad to appear. You now enter you only want this ad to display on people's Facebook pages who have put their current company's name as Museum of Modern Art. Whammo! You just got a backdoor entry to connecting with people you need to connect with: those on the inside of your dream company. The more specific and targeted the ad, the better; you can make it not only appear for the company name, but also only for people who work in your hometown, or from your alma mater. The more generic it is, the more expensive it will be, as the ad will appear on more pages. Try to make it as targeted as possible to make your ad work the best and to save you money.

When job hunting, you are constantly selling yourself. The way you look can have a big im-

Salary Science

pact on how well your sales pitch goes. Science proves that your appearance is a huge contributing factor to making a bigger salary too. A Rice University study[1] found attractive people are considered more trustworthy. Research[2] by Daniel S. Hamermesh and Jeff E. Biddle concluded that attractive women make 4 percent more money than unattractive women. But it's more of a swing for men, as attractive men make 9 percent more money than unattractive men. So hit the beauty parlor and start manscaping; it could end up paying you more than just compliments.

However, attractive women may want to stop short of putting their pretty photo on their resume or LinkedIn profile. Two Ariel University Center economists found[3] that attractive women in Europe and Israel who included a photo with their resume reduced their chances of employment by 20–30 percent. The study speculated that this is because most recruiters are women in these countries. Female recruiters perceived a more attractive woman as a potential threat and may harbor feelings of jealously which hindered the attractive women's chances of getting hired. Personally, in the United States I have mostly experienced male recruiters, so I would imagine the opposite may hold true here. However unfair it is to be judged for your looks, take the research for what is; your appearance will definitely help or hinder you.

9

Goal Line Pay Day

That's what I am now, a rich prick.
Prick always follows the word rich.
Just like schmuck always follows the
word poor.

—Larry David

I did it! Okay, don't hate me just because I've achieved happiness with my six-figure pay day along with a career I'm actually enjoying. I did come from the deepest depths of financial breakdown to get here. Remember when you used to have some sympathy for me? Okay, I don't mean to gloat. I'm taking the time to share my experience so you know all your extra work you are doing now really is worth it. It's hard work, it's uncomfortable, and it can be depressing, but plow through. Find a way. You will thank me later.

It took a variety of ways for me to get to where I am today. A significant factor was taking every obstacle and turning it into an opportunity to learn. Along the way I learned what it is that I want to do, and now, I'm also compensated very well for it. Every change at work, every extra assignment, and every new skill learned was a potential insight on how to better my workplace situation. Maybe it would open new doors, or create a new career path, or confirm I'm doing things just right. Will I do project management forever? Knowing me, probably not. But it is what I want to do now. Saying I'm doing something I want to do is the best feeling in the world. When you want to do something, you are motivated to put in the extra effort. Because I wanted to do project management, that made earning certifications, networking, A/B testing, resume-sniping, working with a ton of different recruiters, changing my approach when I was getting ignored, and all the other little things not feel like work anymore. It just felt necessary. It had to be done to get to where I wanted to be.

I hope you comprehend no one is going to give a job, much less a six-figured salaried one, to someone who isn't willing to put in any extra effort. To maintain employment, I know I have to continue to exceed expectations. I figure that is what I'm being paid to do. I'll do everything I possibly can to not squander my nicely rebuilt life. Once again, I worked hard to get here. I appreciate it much more this time around.

In the end, my career journey lasted four years. The first half was my downfall and the second half was my climb back up. I take nothing for granted anymore financially, and I don't make excuses anymore for my finances either. It's on me to improve my lot in life, regardless of the economy, my skill set, or my education. Blaming others didn't help. Blaming me didn't help. Accepting the situation and creating a plan did help. I didn't want any regrets for not trying everything I could do to get what I wanted. I tried everything. Ultimately, it took doing what was uncomfortable for me. Great things always come when you do. I had to put my neck out there and face rejection (as well as just being ignored) time and time again. But I was up against others who were doing extra work to be noticed. In response, I had to be subversive to get noticed, not only while job hunting, but then again once I was on the job. And then I'd rinse and repeat.

Maybe your goals are different. Maybe you want to make $50,000. Or maybe you just want to find a job. Maybe it will take you five months to get there. Or five years. Remember, it's not how much you make or how fast you make it. (Actually a couple studies[1] show that making between $50,000 and $75,000 is the sweet spot for happiness. Making more than that does not make a person happier.) What matters is that you are doing what you want to do and that you are getting paid at least what you are worth. With the right moves, you can make yourself employable and in demand with even the thinnest resume. If you are not currently happy with your career, then take control of it and make some changes. I agree with Bill Clinton when he said "the price of doing the same old thing is far higher than the price of change."[2] If you keep doing what you are doing now, you'll continue to get the same results. The simple act of creating your own career niche is a low cost change with a potentially huge pay day. What's stopping you from being the expert you were meant to be?

I know you can't follow my exact steps, but maybe I've given you the tools or confidence to at least ask for a raise. Maybe I've given you the motivation to research alternative careers. Maybe I've gotten you to set some goals to put you on a path to riches. Maybe you've learned how to make your job search not only more efficient, but more effective. My insider information on how to get noticed, get ahead, and get a job are proven to work. It's now on you to be subversive too.

As for me, my parting words in this book are going to be more carefully thought out than they were in my last book. I hope I've had my last serving of crow. I'm in a good place now, worked hard to get here, and never gave up until I reached my goals. Everyone has that in them with the right mindset. You know what, after thinking about where it has led me, crow can taste alright when you marinate it for about four years. Maybe my next book will be a cookbook.

Notes

Introduction

1. The Edward Bulwer-Lytton novel *Paul Clifford* began with the infamous line below, greatly panned by his critics and peers: "It was a dark and stormy night; the rain fell in torrents—except at occasional intervals, when it was checked by a violent gust of wind which swept up the streets (for it is in London that our scene lies), rattling along the housetops, and fiercely agitating the scanty flame of the lamps that struggled against the darkness."

There is now an annual Bulwer-Lytton Fiction Contest to come up with the worst opening line to a novel. Jack Barry of Shelby, NC was a 2011 award winner with this entry: "From the limbs of ancient live oaks moccasins hung like fat black sausages—which are sometimes called boudin noir, black pudding or blood pudding, though why anyone would refer to a sausage as pudding is hard to understand and it is even more difficult to divine why a person would knowingly eat something made from dried blood in the first place—but be that as it may, our tale is of voodoo and foul murder, not disgusting food."

Chapter 1

1. Jason M. Fletcher, "Adolescent Depression and Adult Labor Market Outcomes," The National Bureau of Economic Research. www.nber.org/papers/w18216.pdf.

2. Steven Stack, Wayne State University and Jim Gundlach, Auburn University, "The Effect of Country Music on Suicide." http://sf.oxfordjournals.org/content/71/1/211.

3. Galen V. Bodenhausen, Monika A. Bauer, James E. B. Wilkie, and Jung K. Kim, "Consumerism and its antisocial effects can be turned on—or off," *Psychological Science*. *www.psychologicalscience.org/index.php/news/releases/consumerism-and-its-antisocial-effects-can-be-turned-onor-off.html*

4. Leaf Van Boven and Thomas Gilovich, "To Do or to Have? That Is the Question," *Journal of Personality and Social Psychology* Vol 85(6), Dec 2003, 1193-1202. *www.psych.cornell.edu/sec/pub-People/tdg1/VB_&_Gilo.pdf*

5. Thomas DeLeire and Ariel Kalil, "Does consumption buy happiness? Evidence from the United States," *International Review of Economics*. *www.happinesseconomics.net/ocs/index.php/heirs/relationalgoods/paper/viewFile/118/72.*

6. Michael Norton, "How to buy happiness," TEDX talk. *www.ted.com/talks/michael_norton_how_to_buy_happiness.html*.

Chapter 2

1. Charlie Hoehn, Recession Proof Graduate. *www.slideshare.net/choehn/recessionproof-graduate-1722966.*

2. "Keeping an Eye on Recruiter Behavior," TheLadders.com *http://cdn.theladders.net/static/images/basicSite/pdfs/TheLadders-EyeTracking-StudyC2.pdf*.

3. Susan Britton Whitcomb, *Resume Magic: Trade Secrets of a Professional Resume Writer*, 2nd Edition, (Indianapolis, Ind.: JIST Works, 2003).

4. "Findings of 2011 Global Career Brainstorming Day: Trends for the Now, the New & the Next in Careers," Career Thought Leaders Consortium. *www.careerthoughtleaders.com/ wp-content/up/CTL-Brainstorming-WhitePaper-2011.pdf.*

Chapter 3

1. Todd J. Thorsteinson, "Initiating Salary Discussions With an Extreme Request: Anchoring Effects on Initial Salary Offers," *Journal of Applied Social Psychology*. *http://onlinelibrary.wiley.com/ doi/10.1111/j.1559-1816.2011.00779.x/abstract.*

2. Amy Cuddy, "Your body language shapes who you are," *www.ted.com/talks/amy_cuddy_ your_body_language_shapes_who_you_are.html.*

3. "Researchers measure the value of a smile," Phys.org. *http://phys.org/news/2011-05-researchers-measure-the-value-of.html.*

4. "Want a pay raise? Keep on the right side of your boss," Association for Psychological Science. *www.psychologicalscience.org/index.php/ news/want-a-pay-raise-keep-on-the-right-side-of-your-boss.html#.UJJ2em_A9M4.*

Chapter 4

1. Nancy M. Carter and Christine Silva, "The Myth of the Ideal Worker: Does Doing All The Right Things Really Get Women Ahead?" Catalyst. www.catalyst.org/publication/509/the-myth-of-the-ideal-worker-does-doing-all-the-right-things-really-get-women-ahead.

2. Debra Ness, "When Women Do Better, Families Do Better and the Nation Can Thrive," National Partnership for Women & Families, April 12, 2011 http://blog.nationalpartnership.org/index.php/2011/04/when-women-do-better-families-do-better.

3. Ken Auletta, "A Woman's Place," New Yorker July 11, 2011. www.newyorker.com/reporting/2011/07/11/110711fa_fact_auletta?currentPage=1.

4. Shankar Vedantam, "Salary, Gender and the Social Cost of Haggling," Washington Post July 30, 2007. www.washingtonpost.com/wp-dyn/content/article/2007/07/29/AR2007072900827.html.

5. Ernesto Reuben, "Confidence Game," Ideas at Work, Columbia Business School, November 22, 2011 www4.gsb.columbia.edu/ideasatwork/feature/7224716/Confidence+Game.

Chapter 5

1. Greg McKeown, "The Disciplined Pursuit of Less," *Harvard Business Review* August 8, 2012. http://blogs.hbr.org/cs/2012/08/the_disciplined_ pursuit_of_less.html.

2. Robert Oak, "Automated Job Rejection," *The Economic Populist* June 8, 2012. www.economicpopulist.org/content/ automated-job-rejection.

3. "Study finds business school research raises students' salaries," Phys.org, January 24, 2011. http://phys.org/news/2011-01-business-school- students-salaries.html.

4. Anneli Rufus, "15 Signs You Will Be Rich," *The Daily Beast* October 25, 2010. www.businessinsider.com/15-signs-you-will-be- rich-2010-10.

5. "Disadvantaged students reap most finan- cial return from college education, study finds." Phys.Org, April 1, 2010. http://phys.org/ news189317550.html.

Chapter 6

1. Because I like challenges, I've constrained myself from using the last letter of the alphabet throughout the entire book (except when required in the citations). Such a constraint is an example of a lipogram, and you hold in your hands the first non-fiction lipogram ever published! (This is exciting to only me and possibly Jeff Bezos, whose perfect quote was too painful to replace just because of his last name.)

2. Carla Fried, "Make your job really pay," CNN/Money, June 28, 2012. hhttp://money.cnn.com/2012/06/25/pf/job-net-worth.moneymag/index.htm.

3. Anneli Rufus, "15 Signs You Will Be Rich," *The Daily Beast* October 25, 2010. www.businessinsider.com/15-signs-you-will-be-rich-2010-10#people-who-were-popular-in-high-school-earn-10-percent-more-than-people-who-werent-3.

4. Peter Kuhn and Catherine Weinberger, "Leadership Skills and Wages," University of California, Santa Barbara. www.econ.ucsb.edu/~pjkuhn/Research%20Papers/Leader.pdf.

5. Del Jones, "Study says flirtatious women get fewer raises, promotions," *USA Today* August 5, 2005. http://usatoday30.usatoday.com/money/workplace/2005-08-04-sex-usat_x.htm.

6. Lia Samson, "Sleep deprivation can influence professional behavior," Phys.org, August 8, 2012 http://phys.org/news/2012-08-deprivation-professional-behavior.html.

7. "Swearing at Work Can Harm Your Career Prospects, Finds CareerBuilder Survey," CareerBuilder.com, July 25, 2012. www.careerbuilder.com/share/aboutus/pressreleasesdetail.aspx?sd=7/25/2012&id=pr709&ed=12/31/2012.

8. "UI study finds abusive bosses don't suffer for their behavior, if they produce," The University of Iowa News Services, February 4, 2010. http://news-releases.uiowa.edu/2010/february/020410abusivebosses.html.

Chapter 7

1. David Schepp, "Americans Leave Average Of 11 Unused Vacation Days On The Table," AOL Jobs, November 15, 2011. http://jobs.aol.com/articles/2011/11/15/americans-leave-average-of-11-unused-vacation-days-on-the-table.

2. Amanda L. Chan, "Exercise Makes Us Happy—It's Science," Huffington Post February 9, 2012. www.huffingtonpost.com/2012/02/09/exercise-happy-enthusiasm-excitement_n_1263345.html.

3. Torbjörn Vestberg, Roland Gustafson, Liselotte Maurex, Martin Ingvar, and Predrag Petrovic, "Executive Functions Predict the Success of Top-Soccer Players," PLoS ONE 7(4): e34731. doi:10.1371/journal.pone.0034731. www.plosone.org/article/info%3Adoi%2F10.1371%2Fjournal.pone.0034731.

4. M.E. Hopkins, F.C. Davis, M.R. Vantieghem, P.J. Whalen, and D.J. Bucci, "Differential effects of acute and regular physical exercise on cognition and affect," Department of Psychological and Brain Sciences, Dartmouth College. www.ncbi.nlm.nih.gov/pubmed/22554780.

5. Jack Hough, "Want a 9% Raise? Hit the Gym," SmartMoney, June 6, 2012. http://blogs.smartmoney.com/advice/2012/06/06/want-a-9-raise-hit-the-gym.

6. Anneli Rufus, "15 Signs You Will Be Rich," The Daily Beast October 25, 2010. www.businessinsider.com/15-signs-you-will-be-rich-2010-10#nonsmokers-net-worth-is-about-50-percent-higher-than-that-of-light-smokers-and-more-than-twice-as-much-as-that-of-heavy-smokers-13.

7. Bethany L. Peters, PhD and Edward P. Stringham, PhD, "No Booze? You May Lose: Why Drinkers Earn More Money Than Nondrinkers," Reason Foundation, September 2006. http://reason.org/files/42af0a281133fdcfaec166fe7318b57f.pdf.

Chapter 8

1. Rick K. Wilson and Catherine C. Eckel, "Judging a Book by its Cover: Beauty and Expectations in the Trust Game," *Political Research Quarterly* Vol. 59, No. 2 (June 2006). http://rkw.rice.edu/articles/Wilson_Eckel_PRQ_2006.pdf.

2. Daniel S. Hamermesh and Jeff E. Biddle, "Beauty and the Labor Market," *The American Economic Review* Volume 84, Issue 5 (December 1994), 1174-1194. https://webspace.utexas.edu/hamermes/www/BeautyAER94.pdf.

3. Bradley J. Ruffle and Ze'ev Shtudiner, "Are Good-Looking People More Employable?" October 2011. http://ssrn.com/abstract=1705244 or http://dx.doi.org/10.2139/ssrn.1705244.

Chapter 9

1. Alden Wicker, "The Price of Happiness: $50,000?" LearnVest.com, April 24, 2012. www.learnvest.com/knowledge-center/the-price-of-happiness-50000-123.

2. Brian Goldsmith, "Indianapolis Colts: The Most Positive Developments of the Colts Offseason," Bleacher Report. http://bleacherreport.com/articles/1260300-indianapolis-colts-the-most-positive-developments-of-the-colts-offseason

Index

Acknowledgments

Writing a book is always a team effort, and I am forever grateful to all that helped get it across the goal line (sports analogy courtesy of my time at ESPN). This book would not have been possible without Gordon Warnock providing support, encouragement, and direction from the proposal stage through the first draft of the manuscript. Thank you for making this project come to life.

Vicki Motter's pitching got this project noticed and in the right hands. Your hard work is very much appreciated.

My family and friend's feedback and support is not unnoticed. My buddies Josephine Imbriani, Matt Kubala,

Jon Marballi, and Carissa Bennett not only provided excellent career advice and motivation, but sparked the idea of this book in the first place.

Rich Webley's connections and recommendation helped catapult me into a new career, and I'll forever be thankful. I will never turn down a night of beers with you.

Many thanks to the Island Skirmish crew, who always know how to keep me humble, even though I'm easily the most handsome, athletic, and talented of them all.

If you've laughed while reading this book, it's probably because Andrew Wright made the funny funnier. If you cried, then you probably got a paper cut (and I would recommend an e-reader). If you're still reading this, then you're probably just looking for your name. (One lucky reader remains!)

So lastly, thank you to my wife, Sadia. Even during an economic rollercoaster, you're steady as a rock—just one of the million and four things I love about you.

About the Author

Alan Corey is a Brooklyn-based entrepreneur, speaker, writer, and the author of *A Million Bucks by 30*. To find out more Alan visit his Website at *www.alancorey.com* or follow him on Twitter at @alancorey.